Rockin' in a Big Rig

—

Grammie's Log

Sarah Weber

Irvine, California

2016

With my truck in Missouri, late 2015.

A preface addressed
to my readers

I write this book to show that at any age one can learn something new. I wanted to see the world or a part of it, God's world that He made for us. I wanted to demonstrate that anything is possible with determination, in my case aided by a trustworthy friend who has helped me from the beginning. I started this adventure late in my life as I had to wait until my divorce was finalized and my kids were grown.

This book is written and published for me and my four children who will find it surprising what their mother did in her old age. Surely some time in ten or twenty years, my grandchildren – six at present – will read my story of what their Grammie did after she became fifty.

The book is also for my friends and fellow-truckers, several of whom have asked if they might have a copy since this log of a few years will show a rare view of a trucker's life, of a person new to this complex business, and especially of a woman's experience. I'm glad to share this story with those who are fascinated by big rigs and the life of a trucker on the road.

I have always admired the traveling of a truck driver, the big rig motor, the sound that a Jake brake* makes when going down a hill, the sights that one might see along the way. It's amazing that we all get everything *from somewhere else. How does it all get to the store where I buy it? Answer: by a truck and its driver.*

As to the origin of my wanting to become a driver of an 18-wheeler, often just called a "big-rig," this ambition can be traced to when husband Larry and I started work on trucks nearly thirty years ago. We did a few show trucks, which is when I really got the bug. There were some really fine looking trucks, decked out nicely.

While I was cleaning the inside and polishing the vinyl, Larry would use a high-speed buffer and polish the fuel tanks, the headache rack**, and the exhaust pipe stacks. When we were finished it was sharp looking. The one show truck we did, won a prize.

My appreciation for truckers was strengthened by one incident in 1987 when my daughters Sharon and Natalie were just under two years old. A very bad day in my Fresno life turned out in positive shape with a trucker helping save me. I went to a Fresno truck stop to have one of the truckers take me and my two girls to my parents. I used the C.B. and I asked truckers in the Central Valley for help.

A man called back and told me he had to talk to his wife first. The couple had a 6 month old son. And shortly he called to have the three of us meet them at the restaurant in an hour. And they let us stay with them for a few months in their Fresno home until I found a route back into my safe happy life. That trucking couple were absolutely 100% my lifesavers.

My trucking story in these chapters is a record of exactly what it's like for a middle-aged woman to start in on a trucking career and to spend years earning a living by driving a big rig. The text provides a log of where and how I went on the nation's highways, picking up and delivering loads in much of the United States.

Now, sit back and enjoy the story of my exploits, while I roll it. Hope you shall enjoy reading of my daily life, with the illustrations and other info to show you a real trucker's life on the open road.

*Jacobs Engine Brake, this is a
     secondary braking system on large diesel trucks.
** Headache rack for a flatbed or step deck trailer,
     to protect the cabin's rear window.

Table of Contents

Chapter 1:
Truck Driving School - Training and Road Testing.

This line of work has been in the back of my mind for many years. It has become much more appealing than the various jobs I've had in the past. So I am taking the plunge – enrolling in school.

On Facebook I shall write my children and a few friends daily notes of my experiences. Or at least occasional notes of what I'm doing, where I'm going, what I've seen on the road, and some of the ups and downs and pleasures of this line of work. It's an exciting venture to choose a very demanding and exciting career as a long-haul truck driver.

February 2013 – I am with my boyfriend Twisten, a truck driver for thirty two years. He is teaching me a lot about what I would be doing as a truck driver. Twisten wants to help me with a school and get hired with a company that would hire just-licensed drivers.

April 29, 2013 – As for my first day of school, it was a lot of testing. To see what I know and what the instructor needs to go over with me. I'm the only student for the day class and there are two in the afternoon class. Took my DOT (Department of Transportation) green card medical test, and a drug test as well. I have a booklet to study.

May 15, 2013 – First time doing parallel parking – and I did it! And a picture proves it!!

June 13, 2013 – My education is ongoing from Truck Driver Institute, located in Santa Maria. The day before yesterday I drove on freeway 101 for the first time. It's just not easy when we don't get much time on the truck, about an hour if that ... mostly three days a week, since the truck is always being used for testing. I was going to try to graduate on the 18th, as my teacher wanted me too. But then he and I talked, as I didn't feel comfortable yet to take my DMV test to graduate. So he is going to let me continue for the next three weeks, and try then. That did not work out.

July 31, 2013 – Thursday I will be moving to Dootson Truck Drive School to test-drive one of their trucks, as  they have a fleet of day cabs with short (27 foot) trailers. My boyfriend is paying $500 for three hours driving and one DMV test drive. He feels as I do about my school schedule since I failed my first drive test. I have been only getting 20-30 minutes with the teacher each week. Plus the previous school only had one working truck for the test, and to me it seemed to need the clutch fixed.

2

August 6, 2013 –I didn't go for the driving test. I canceled it yesterday. I need to know more to be more comfortable, like stopping distance, when to up shift and down shift, get better at holding the clutch with one foot and the brake with the other. Listening to the engine when it revs up to shift gear properly. I just need more time behind the wheel to do better. I just don't want to feel so scared behind the wheel in such a big rig and have to think about so much, even other drivers or pedestrians as well. I would just cry if I don't pass I've come so far.

October 2013 – Time for a change. I took truck-driving school lessons, first with the Dootson School of Trucking with better equipment. I passed the pre-trip and the skills tests. Just didn't pass the driving part, because I had the gear shifter switch on the high side, not the low side. I have a learning disability so it takes me longer than the average person to do the driving test. I've never driven a stick shift before I got into a big rig, so it's like a teacher helping me learn dance steps.

The financing of school comes through a Federal program which covers all tuition costs. I continue to pay my housing, food, and other personal routine expenses such as driving to and from the school which is located miles from Arroyo Grande in San Luis Obispo County and thus I have mounting out-of-pocket expenses during the school.

ZERO TUITION $2995 **CDL TRAINING** VALUE!
PLUS EMPLOYMENT UPON COMPLETION   "If you don't have a class A CDL, we've got you covered. With partner schools located throughout the U.S., we offer the chance to get your license with ZERO TUITION with a nine month employment commitment. On top of that, once you finish truck driving school and upon meeting our hiring criteria, we guarantee employment with our company."

I then was guided to another school where I finally completed school driving lessons with C.R. England at a

Fontana facility, a company with headquarters in West Valley City, Utah. I stayed there nights at the Red Tile Inn, spending weekends visiting with my daughter Sharon to shorten the drive to and from the school.

C.R. England lists the following truck driver school requirements:

Have a satisfactory three-year employment record.

Have a clean driving record.

Pass a mandatory drug screen.

Be able to pass a Department of Transportation physical
    from a doctor at the direction of C.R. England.

Results of the physical that meet minimum standards, including:

    A blood pressure rating of 140/90 or less.

    An eyesight rating of 20/40 or better.

    A horizontal field of vision rating of no less than 80 degrees.

Pass a C.R. England road test.

Understand that firearms are strictly forbidden on C.R. England
    property.

Meet criminal record policy requirements.

And C.R. England promotes its school in this way:- "Time spent in the trucks will teach you how to: Turn the tractor-trailer. Handle railroad crossings and intersections. Drive in city and highway traffic. Back up the tractor-trailer. Couple and uncouple the tractor to the trailer. Inspect your equipment, including the complete pre-trip inspection. Test your brakes."

Oct. 9, 2013 – I was outside in the soaking rain freezing. Waiting all day to get in a truck to do an alley docking skill and never got a chance for 12 hours. Only got to study the pre-trip inspection that I've been studying last week. As soon as I got back to the hotel I made some soup and hot chocolate to warm up some. Tonight (in an hour) I will take a hot shower and go straight to bed. I go to bed at 8:30 p.m.

and wake up at 3:30 a.m. we have school from 5:30 a.m. to 5 p.m. every day. As soon as my head hits the pillow I'm out like a light. It used to take me an hour just lying in bed before I fall asleep. Now I'm just plum tired.

Later I report: Tomorrow we get our trainers that will give us more time driving and doing the backing skills that we must be ready to do by Tuesday or Wednesday. If I don't pass I have to wait two days to test again. But if I pass I will go with another driver who will train me on the road for either 30 days or 20,000 miles, whichever comes first that is called phase one. I don't know what phase two is yet.

I have been sexually harassed by two guys at the school already. I've had to tell them to stop a few times. Now they are leaving me alone. As I've had to walk away from them once they start walking towards me and start talking to me. I told the security guy about it and he said if it happens again, I will make a formal report. But other than that, it's been good. Well, now it's time for me to take my hot shower and get some sleep.

I have two female roommates I'm sharing the room with. These two ladies are in the class ahead of me by one week. They failed their test for the DMV yesterday, so they test tomorrow. If they pass, then I might have them a few more days before they head out on their 30 days or 20,000 miles. Then I might get two new female roommates from the week behind my class to share the room with them during their training.

Each week there is a new class that starts. It was 100 students, now down to 65 in just my class alone. Anyhow I enjoyed the rain but not the freezing wind.

Oct. 17 – I wrote my parents and brothers my big news:

Sarah did it today!

I passed the California Commercial Driver's License to handle big rigs. And I was hired!

On the next page is the picture of me this day of 2013 celebrating my achievement with my very good and skilled school instructor.

Oct. 20 - First day on the job... I drove 502.1 miles today...I'm good! I love this job! So peaceful, and quite, just God and I on the road...just what I prayed for.

Oct. 21 - I'm now a Mother Trucker. All I know is that I will be with another Mentor/trainer for either one month or 20,000 miles whichever is first. That's phase 1. Then I go for an upgrade, and then phase 2 team driving 2 weeks or 10,000 miles. Then I go to Utah and get keys to my own truck. I want to go all over the 48 states.

Nov. 25, 2013 – I report to my family and parents that I had passed the next major hurdle as I embark on my career.

"I passed my upgrade!"

--0-0-0-0-0--

C.R. England training is described and defined and explained in this way:-

"Upon successful completion of your schooling and upon meeting our hiring requirements, you will be hired and provided with paid on-the-job training with a professional trainer. Your training and team driving will take place in two phases and insures that you receive the most comprehensive training in the industry.

Phase I "Phase I training consists of team driving with a professional trainer for a minimum of 20,000 miles or 30 Days of being under Dispatch. During this time you will complete three (3) training modules.

Phase 2 - Team Driving/ Second Seat "During team driving, drivers will team with either a Company First Seat

7

Trainer or an Independent Contractor. During this time you will further your education with the completion of three self-guided training modules.

"Once you begin team driving you will be able to request home time. C.R. England values the work/family balance of our drivers and we will make every effort to get you home within two weeks of your request.

"Once you have completed your training program you can choose from the following possibilities. 1) Become a Company Solo or Team driver and receive a steady income with a stable company. 2) Buy or Lease your own truck and become an Independent Contractor running your own business. Or 3) Remain as a second seat.

"After successful completion of the C.R. England truck driving training course and upon meeting our hiring requirements, you will be hired, receive your California CDL (Commercial Driver's License), and be assigned to a certified Over-the-Road Driver Trainer. With your trainer, you will be given opportunities to gain a personal understanding of your new career and have the valuable information you learned in class reinforced through first-hand driving experience."

--o-o-o-o-o--

I have nine months to work and thereby repay the school costs that had been prepaid by US government training program.

If I leave the company short of the nine months, I must pay the full balance out of my own pocket. So working until at least July 17th 2014 is a target for me.

I started driving with a mentor in November 2013, trucking to drop-off cities all over the US, to achieve 20,000 miles after which I shall be licensed for solo driving and then gets keys to my own C.R. England truck.

8

Nov. 28, 2013 – Good morning from Arizona, and a happy Thanksgiving.

I'm on the road heading to Missouri. I've got my next phase with a new trainer and he will be picking me up in a few days, so enjoy Thanksgiving without me.

The road training has begun – My first mentor was a woman about age 49. She has only been driving one and a half years. I should have gotten 20,000 miles or 30 days - whichever comes first. I only made 15,000 miles in 30 days.

Then to upgrade from Phase I, I have to drive the truck around town, and demonstrate my backing up skill, to show I'm much better.

9

Chapter 2:- Cross Country with a Mentor.

Nov. 29, 2013 – Good Morning America. My mentor driver and I are today heading out East from Denver Colorado. I loved Utah. I drove through Colorado and Kansas, in Missouri now (sunset in MO below). Working toward East coast ... but I found out we'll be heading south ... to Texas.

Dec. 3 – Leaving Georgia, heading to Kansas.

I wish I had money now...I'm starving! And haven't bought a shower in a week. Not enough points on my card to take a shower. So I'm doing the best that I can until the money gets rolling in.

Dec. 7 - Ice on the windshield too. What do I do? Just trying to stay warm trucking on the road. Scary in winter driving when the trailer is sliding. It's getting worse out here...no reason to drive right now. Anyone else can be the fool...but not I.

My load can wait. Staying in Moriarty, New Mexico, for the night, winter storm making it unsafe to drive. Zero visible conditions. Storm should be blowing over.   There are bunk beds called sleepers where we sleep, no kitchen, no bathrooms. Two people take turns driving is a team. We take shifts. One sleeps; the other drives. When the weather becomes too bad, we pull over to the nearest truck stop or rest area to stay. Right now we are at a truck stop so we can use the bathroom, and get food and water. We also have 3-days of food on the truck. We have a bunk heater that will keep us warm. But I have a sleeping bag. Plus Long Johns to keep me warm.

Dec. 12, 2013 – From Wells to Reno, driving across Nevada...pretty snow on mountains. It was very cold too. I've been to Arizona, New Mexico, Tennessee, Arkansas, Nevada, Idaho, Colorado, Texas, Georgia, Louisiana, Mississippi, Missouri, Oklahoma, in just the last two weeks, during Phase II training. Now heading to Florida. It's a dream come true for me. To get paid to travel. It's a paid vacation – for now just earning eleven cents a driven mile. Now I am leaving Reno on way to Utah. For a month, I was with my first mentor, Luanna, who has been driving a year and a half. We mostly ran on highway 10, very boring road across the country.

Dec. 13 – After a day and a half waiting in Utah, I'm now on my way to Orlando, Florida, C.R. England has sent me out with this  trainer mentor, heading to the East coast, with a 21-year-old named Randy who has been driving 5 months. I'm teaching him things about trucking, when he should be teaching me. I have to get 5,000 -10,000 miles. That should equal 30,000 total miles I've driven, not total miles the truck does. I have 6,000 more miles to go. Then I prove to the company again that I can take their drive test and pass. Then I will get keys to my own truck – an upgrade from Phase II.

Dec. 14 – I left my folks in California a phone message: "Coughing, sneezing, body aches, headaches, I feel miserable in Missouri. Achoo, good night all." And the next day late evening, sounding dreadful, I talked with my mother by phone from Georgia and heading to Florida.

Dec. 16 - In Orlando, Florida, I'm at the hospital having a hard time breathing, sneezing, coughing, body aches, headache. All I want to do is sleep. But No! Well, I got the x-ray done, now just waiting for them to call my name. Later the doctor said it's viral. Not pneumonia. I will get a breathing treatment, cough medicine, nose stuff too. I'm good! Yeah!!! After about 8 hours in the hospital, I phone my parents to report progress, saying that it was a virus with chest cold, and I was given two prescriptions to fill at a cost of $137. I've lost more weight...I'm now 168 pounds...I guess it pays to be sick. My skinny jeans are too big for me.

Dec. 16 - I and Randy are waiting in Orlando now for assignment of our next pickup. Most loads are "cold," using trailer refrigeration, and may be meats, diary or vegetables. Occasionally we deliver "dry" loads.

Dec. 17 – Waiting for assignment, and passing by Universal Orlando Resort today.

Dec. 19 – Man, Florida is a toll money-hungry State! I can't wait to get out of here!!! We are sent a message to the truck to let us know where we get the loads and where they must be delivered to. Then, once delivered, they might get us a near-by load to somewhere else. Never knowing any sooner where we or I am going.

Dec. 20 – Heading to Oregon. Left Florida, good morning Georgia. …. Good evening Kentucky; on my way to Oregon and it's my turn to drive.

Dec. 21 – In Idaho heading to Oregon, then another load in Washington to Tennessee. Goodbye to Nebraska hello Wyoming. Oh my God! Thank you Lord for helping me drive the truck into 50  mile gusting high winds, snow covered roads where you can't see the ground or lines. I drove slow, with my hazard lights on going 15 miles per hour on the freeway that was posted at 75 MPH. Thank God I survived. This was during the night, not being able to see the road lines, and the windshield was covered with snow no much it is called "white out" I'm at a Travel Centers of America truck stop, safe and sound. Highway 80 in Wyoming. I'd never driven

in the snow before. Temperature was 16° so the snow didn't stick to the ground. Wyoming, good bye. Beautiful place...but scary!

Dec. 22 – I've reached Oregon. I love the rain, snow, people, climate too. Paula and her husband both drive a beautiful big rig named "Mutt Hut" - with their little dog. Met them at a rest stop then at a truck stop in Oregon. Now it's very late evening in Troutdale, Oregon. Good night all. Unloading in Othello, WA, in the morning.

Dec. 24 – Early morning picking up the next load to take to Smyma, Tennessee. (That gets me ready for the C.R. England "upgrade" review, which can be done in one of three sites.) Mid-evening: "Good night Montana, merry Christmas Eve everyone, honk honk honk."

Dec. 25 – "Merry Christmas all, please pray for us truck drivers that still are working, like me. I wish I could be at home with family and friends" as I am driving through Moorcroft, in extreme Northeastern Wyoming on the banks of the Belle Fourche River. Then driving through South Dakota at noon. "Seeing the country! Pretty cool? It is ... it's a paid vacation! Or a paid tourist!"

15

Dec. 27 –Arkansas, getting ready to drop this load late morning. Waiting to get this Freightliner unloaded. Then pick up next load for Texas.

Dec. 29 - Across from a truck stop, in a Ramada Inn, in southern Dallas, TX, motel, put there by C.R. England after I reported to the company "Safety" office that I would no longer drive with my young trainer Randy, since he at times drives too fast, erratically, and very dangerously. He drove in an urban area where trucks are not authorized, and had the truck stuck in an intersection from which he could not maneuver to get out of the jam, and he then asked me to wake up and take over the controls. He seems too inexperienced to serve as a skilled qualified driver – to say nothing of being my "trainer."

Picture is at a truck stop - well after my lunch finished on the 27th .

C.R. England accepted my reports, asked me to file a detailed statement, and to drive with Randy to the next drop in Michigan. I dislike continuing with Randy. The company is determining my next assignment.

Dec. 30 – Still waiting. Then late afternoon a call from C.R. England in Fontana comes to give me information of what's ahead. "I'm in south Dallas. I just found out, I have enough miles to upgrade and get keys to my own truck...happy dance time. Just not sure when that will happen as it is the holidays. Maybe get my truck here to take back to California for home time. Or drive with another driver and share the driving to California. I will get more information tomorrow (keeping my fingers crossed).

Not been home for four months. I need my home time. I need to meet my new granddaughter." I spoke to the safety manager and again reported that I didn't feel safe with this young kid as my Mentor. The man I spoke with finally agreed with me and let me stay at a hotel in Dallas, Texas. I packed all my stuff and nicely said my goodbye to my mentor

Dec. 31 – I'm on the phone with my company. Driver Manager said that there were sensors on that truck that would have backed up what I said. But there weren't any red flags. So they can't get me a truck to ride on to get me to a place to upgrade. I'm stuck here...because they said there isn't a load going from Dallas to California. I might have to jump on a truck to go upgrade in Burns Harbor or at Salt Lake.

Late afternoon:- called mother with the good news that I'm on a truck with Randy #2 and another driver: – "Good news!!! They found a truck that will take me back today to Mira Loma (near Fontana, ca. 50 miles SSW of Hesperia). Happy dance!!!!" [Next morning] Good morning Arizona, almost to California!

17

Trucker's jokes are of all types. I've heard a ton. Every major interstate trucking company is given an acronym by truckers, this being -

"What Does ENGLAND Stand For?

Every New Guy Leaves After Ninety Days"

Jan. 4, 2014 - Home to check on my apartment in Arroyo Grande, to see if everything was alright. It was. Now I went to the hotel and got my room for the weekend and then go to Fontana on Monday at 6 am for my "upgrade" and hopefully get keys to my own truck.

Then after I'm finished with School, I plan on taking some time off to visit Nick and his family, Sharon and her family. And spend some time relaxing, and maybe visiting friends. Before I go trucking again.

Jan. 6 - I passed all my written tests, now tomorrow I get to test drive for them. Once that is done I will find out about getting a truck and where. (With Phase II "upgrade," I qualify to be a solo driver, with much improved pay.)

Jan. 7 - I'm so excited! I just have to do forward drive, no backing. I put my name down for a dedicated run. (It just means I will be running 6 weeks and have 4 days off. But it will be from central USA to Oakland, California flip. Right now it's a solo run but with the option to train another student to run teams.)

I will need a TWIC card to go to Oakland port from central USA. The Transportation Worker Identification Credential (or TWIC) program is a US Transportation Security Administration and U.S. Coast Guard initiative. The TWIC program provides a tamper-resistant biometric credential to maritime workers requiring unescorted access to secure Port areas handling international shipments.

18

Jan. 8, 2014 - I pray I get that job.... Great News - I PASSED!!! ... happy dance time! Here is the Training Program certificate I received today.

Midafternoon:- *I got the job*.

It's going to wait for me to take 'home time,' so I can visit my granddaughter. I will be gone six weeks on the road driving solo and then home four days.

The open roads beckon.

Chapter 3:- Driving Solo on Dedicated Runs.

Jan. 14, 2014 – It is official:- I pick up check tomorrow morning, at the yard...yeah!!! I'm a busy woman, got to keep moving. If the wheels ain't turning then I ain't making any money. Let's have some fun!!! Oh wait...I can't. I have to get to bed. Got a drive of 6 hours to get my big rig ... nighty nite all.

Jan. 15 - I'm here at C.R. England Yard in Mira Loma, CA. Now where is my truck .... Here! My clean truck, dated from 2012....it's going in the shop to be serviced. [Late afternoon:-] Sleeping in my red truck #59161 and having it serviced before my load tomorrow.

Jan. 16 - I drove down to Mira Loma yard yesterday. I slept on the truck last night. I had the truck serviced at the shop, then had to get the papers like registration, tags and stickers put on the truck. I go to Fresno to pick up a load and take it to Denver Colorado. Next Monday, 1/20 at 6 a.m., I meet with another driver to teach me how to zip tie (also known as using cable ties) - versatile, durable, highly reliable, releasable, and reusable - to tie securely the container loads that I will be taking. Then I leave for Fresno and stay the night there.

Jan. 17 – I write my folks to fill them in on what's going on:- "I only know that I pick up containers from a place or another driver. Once I get my TWIC card then I will be able to go to ports. Where the ships come in and carry containers from other countries, or I take them to port to be shipped to other countries. It pays a bit more than other sections of this company. But not much to pay the bills just yet. I have more paperwork and other things to do for this type of loads. Plus the TWIC card is a government thing, I get fingerprinted and have a background check done on me. Plus it costs $200 for this card.

Then there is another card for airports called TSA card to pick up and drop off containers at the airports, that card also requires fingerprints and a background check that costs $100. Other solo drivers will get paid 24 cents, I will get 28 cents a mile. So I hope I can make it.

Once I get a few weeks or so going solo, I might become a trainer and train another student like I was, and that pays even more. But first I want to learn how this works for me so I will be able to teach someone else. But for now...I go solo."

Noon: I'm being live-loaded at my pick up in Fresno. Truck lights are not working, "check engine" light came on just after I got the load. There are 7 faults showing, no 4 ways, no turn signals, no cruise control...ugh, this is cutting in my drive time! It's not cool to be stopped for lights. I don't want a ticket, so I'm waiting for road service. Need to turn off battery switch for 2 minutes; then back on to reset the lights. Very late that evening: I made it to Baker, CA. Good night all. Vegas in the morning to see my family. Then off to Denver, Co. I average driving 500 miles each day.

Jan. 18 – When I drove through Las Vegas, I got to see Natalie, Chad, Mac, Melody, and Liberty. I bought them all lunch and showed them my truck and drove them all a bit in the truck stop. They loved it. Plus Natalie gave me my Christmas gift, which was a dragon necklace (I love it!).

My daughter Natalie posts on Facebook: *"MOM came to visit... and showed us her big rig!"*

Jan. 19, late evening:- Second drop in Denver today ... good night all.

I get to wash my truck any time I get to a company yard. I get to wash my truck once every 6 weeks. I wish I could wash it once a week. I wash my own windshield every chance I can at any truck stop to fuel up.

I fuel up at one of these three places, Pilot, Flying J, or Love's. There is NO lock for the fuel caps.

Jan. 20 - Commerce City, CO. Then off at noon to Dodge City KS.

Jan. 21, early morning:- Yard dogs are mean jerks. I ask for help and they all refuse. I just can't get the landing gear up.... It took me an hour to get the landing gear to move.

Jan. 21, 11 pm: -Mom and Dad, I'm in New Mexico at a truck stop in Laguna. I have 782 miles to go to drop this load in Long Beach CA at the pier. I drove today from

Dodge City Kansas, through Oklahoma, Texas, and now in New Mexico for the night. As for stopping by Irvine to see you, I won't know where my next load will take me, as they give me a new load orders when I drop this one. Well it's late and I have to sleep and start early in the morning. Pre-trip inspection, eat, bathroom, and drive...not all in that order...giggles good night. Sarah"

Jan. 22 –I found out I get to drop this container at the Mira Loma yard, another driver will take it as he has the TWIC card I don't have to drop it at the pier. I'm at Flagstaff AZ.

Jan. 23 at C.R. England Yard in Mira Loma, near Fontana in Riverside County. Got to spend some time with my sweetheart, then a few with my daughter Sharon and my grandkids Jessmarr and Alissa, plus my daughter's boyfriend made me some poles to open the container's doors, then my sweetheart fixed them up for me. Also got to see my two other daughters earlier this week, one of whom gave me the dragon necklace I am wearing. This has been a great week. What is next? I get two different things to do. I'm staying put...here!

"Just thought I'd take the time to tell you, I'm no longer with England. ... Why? Because CR England never allowed me to go back home. That was putting my health and safety at risk. And then NO pay....so I called IT quits."

Was driving solo, now I got a co-driver that is great to be with. I'm blessed. My new co-driver Alan was a classmate from C.R. England truck driving school. He is two years younger than me, with family in Nova Scotia, Texas, Boston, and friends all over. Thank you God for my life. Now we're heading to Aurora Colorado, from Moreno Valley, CA.

Jan. 24 – I'm driving a Freightliner model "Cascade 2012" built in Salt Lake, Utah. Viewed on the next page is the sleeping section in the top picture, looking into the front of the cab with driver and passenger seats shown in the lower picture.

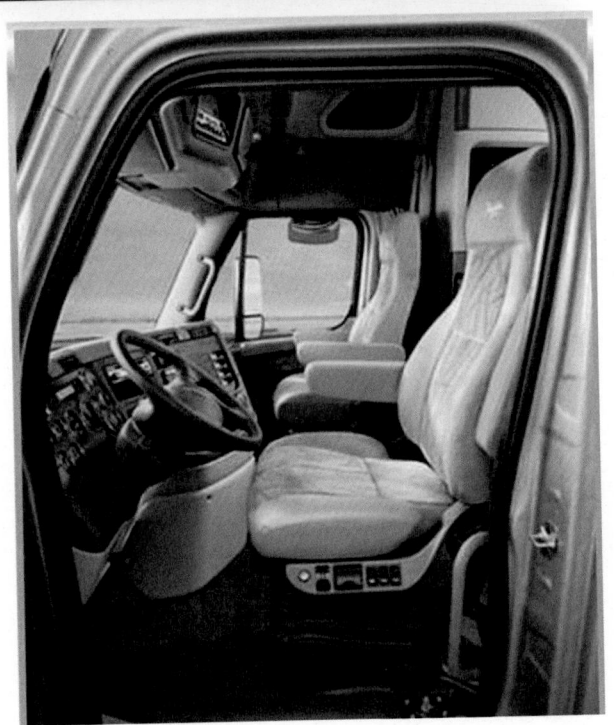

Jan. 27 - to Oakland, to drop this load at California Family Fitness - Sports Complex.

Jan. 28 - Heading to Stockton to pick up a load, then dropping it off in Ogden Utah

Jan. 29 - We drop load at Port of Oakland, Berth 22, Maersk/Horizon Lines Ports of America.

Jan. 30 at 8:12am - Done getting loaded in Idaho, and now off to Brighton, Colorado, to drop this load.

Jan. 31 - I'm in Cheyenne Wyoming. Highway 25 south is closed. Temp. now is -17 degrees. *Cold!* Bedding down at the Flying J. Getting off the I-80 was murder. Made it to our drop at 11:14am.

This sleeping, finding time to sleep well, is a problem I must work on all the time. Here is one very lengthy blog by "Trucker Mike" on this aspect of trucking – and he states it very well.

Sleep Cycle of a Truck Driver - It Doesn't Exist

One thing that I wasn't quite prepared for when I decided to become a truck driver is the sleeping patterns. I knew fatigue was a big issue in truck driving, but now I truly understand why. The long driving hours are only part of the issue. But the main issue is the lack of any normal "bed time" for an OTR truck driver. There is a common saying in the trucking industry, and that is; "drive when you have to, sleep when you can." This phrase is spot on when describing the sleep patterns of a truck driver. And in fact, there really is no pattern.

Having Hours Available on Logbook When You Need 'Em

The situation is a bit complex, but if you want to maintain high miles every week, you need to make yourself available at the right times. Due to the government's hours of service regulations on truck drivers, we must plan ahead, sometimes days in advance, what we will be doing each hour of each day. If we make our delivery at 6 a.m. with no legal driving hours remaining for the next 10 hours, the chances of getting a load at all that day is slim to none, since most shipments are sent out in

26

the morning. So, the trick is to drive a certain cycle, while trying to remain within the legal barriers of the regulations, so that you have full hours available in the mornings.

There Is No Sleep Pattern for Truckers

But unfortunately, as soon as you get into a specific cycle, things change. The trucking industry runs 24/7/365 and so do many shippers and receivers. The last couple weeks have been all over the board for me as far as loading and unloading times at our customers. It was 3 a.m. for a load one day, 2.p.m. the next. A 4 a.m. delivery this day, and a 10 a.m. delivery the next. Not only that, but I've had quite a few loads with multiple stops. This only complicates the issue, because you must be sure to have hours available to make it through all of your deliveries and stay within the legal guidelines. On the surface, it doesn't seem too difficult. But in reality, it is. The planning is one thing, but forcing your body to stay awake or fall sleep at different times every day is another thing. I'm hoping that as I gain more experience, I'll get a little better at my trip planning, and can set up more of a routine. I can tell you for certain, the most widely used drug out here in the trucking industry is caffeine. Walk into any truck stop and go to the front counter. You'll be sure to see several displays of energy drinks, energy shots and even caffeine pills. And my beverage of choice these days is Mountain Dew.

Part of the issue for me lately is I'll drive for 8+ hours to my shipper or receiver for an early 3 a.m. appointment, but I can't sleep yet. I have either to watch the customer load or unload the product, listen for my truck number to be called on the CB, or watch the ever so exciting blinking red light at the dock and wait until it turns green. Many customers do have a "wake up" service, but I haven't had the luxury of going to those customers the last couple weeks. Not only that, but the places I've been lately have taken 4+ hours to get me loaded or unloaded. Once they are finally done, it's time to try and find a parking spot. Late at night, this can be a seemingly impossible task. Truck stops and rest areas are jam packed by nightfall, and it can easily take a couple hours to find somewhere to shut down.

Your "Ten Hour Break" Rarely Means 10 Hours of Sleep

While waiting at the customer to be loaded or unloaded, most drivers log that time in the sleeper berth. Basically, as soon as they show the sleeper berth in their logbook, they are on their "break." Once 10 hours of break time has been reached, they are able to drive again. But as stated before, shippers and receivers can often take 4 hours or more to finish loading or unloading. So that 10 hour break normally reserved for sleeping, quickly turns into 6 hours. Add on another hour to find a *parking spot, another 30 minutes to grab a shower, and maybe if there's time, another 30 minutes to grab a meal. Where did that 10 hour break go? Four hours of sleep is sometimes all you get.*

Feb. 1 – Good morning, all. I'm up and rolling. In Altamont, MO. Going 35 miles an hour. This rig can weigh 80,000 pounds including the cab, trailer and load. Just the cab with sleeper is 12,000 pounds. The sleeper truck has a bunk heater to help one stay warm in cold climates.

Feb. 2 - at the rest stop in Wyoming on the 80...Freezing! Good night in Wells, NV. Heading to Oakland, CA. in the morning. Feb. 3rd - We made it. Safe and sound. Mechanic will look at broken air-line in a few minutes. At the Petro in Sparks. Off the 80. Brakes are NOT holding air. Having it looked at.

Feb.5 - Gosh!!! Just left Oakland, CA. Now near Wadsworth, NV, and returning to Denver, CO. Whaa

Whaa Whaa. It's cold out there! And late evening:- I'm fighting winds and snow and -12° chill. When a Trucker or car flies by me, it blows snow and I can't see the road. I made it to a safe haven. Thank GOD. In Wamsutter, WY, over half way from Salt Lake City to Cheyenne.

Feb. 10 - I've been traveling from Oakland, CA, to Denver, CO. Kansas to Oakland, Milan Missouri to Oakland, driving mostly on the I-70 and I-80. I am in Flagstaff AZ. Heading to San Pedro CA. right now. We haul mostly meat that goes to the port and is shipped to China or Japan, (the list of what kind of cuts of what meat is just a bunch of numbers). When its dry stuff to be sent across the ocean, we are only given numbers. If it's a local run, we get information of what we are carrying.

At first, since Jan 24, co-driver Alan was kind. I shared my

food and water with him. Now he is getting frustrated with my DM ("driver manager") and feels he wants to jump ship from container fleet. He doesn't like all the paperwork that I do for this fleet. He has become more and more hard to live with in a 6'×6' space. He keeps touching me, talking my ear off, and it bothers me. I've told him to stop, and even tell him to get into the sleeper [pictured above] although he doesn't sleep much. He likes to help me by hooking up the trailers to the truck, winding down the landing gear, or up, hooking up the airlines and power line for me. But I never ask him to do that. I've told him I can do it, but he is being a gentleman to the point I can't do my job that I'm paid to do. I fill out the papers, and send messages to our DM.

I'm praying he gets off my truck.) My DM now agrees to get Alan off my truck. Then I will go in for training to become a trainer to other new students. That will pay more if I do that. BTW, I work with three DMs, Ron and Donnie and a woman DM Terra, depending on the time of day or night I need their help.

Feb. 11 - Well, now I'm back to being a solo driver. I'm in Fullerton, CA. Heading to Fountain, Co. I listen to country music while I'm driving. I LOVE the dragon necklace so

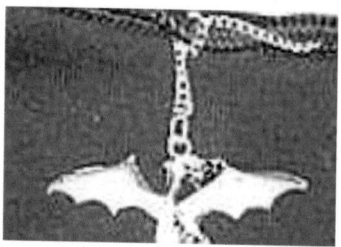

much...it puts a smile on my face every day. And keeps me pushing when I'm scared driving in ice, snow, rain and wind. I also wear a cross I got from South Point Church in Fresno 17 years ago. The

Dragon I got from my dear daughter Natalie Banks for Christmas last year. Thank you so much. As you can tell the necklace is tangled up...as I wear it all the time and rub them both, knowing I'm loved, by God and my children. And a cross protects my spirit while I'm on this earth.

I told my folks that my truck has SiriusXM radio which costs me $155 per year, with no commercials, and I can change stations by just pushing a button.

The truck GPS display is on a 3x4 inch square adhered on the windshield, showing me where I am and where going. I use the *Pocket Truck Stop Guide* 2013 edition, described as "The pocket truck stop guide is designed as a quick reference tool to provide basic transit critical data, i.e. the locations of truck stops in sequential order, the size of parking area and whether or not the facility has a scale or repair facilities. If you are in a storm or dense fog, if you are in a small town and need to find a scale, if you are getting drowsy or you are just plain hungry and need to stop, now you can find the next best place to pull off in a matter of seconds." It's some 150 pages of very useful and essential info for about $10.

Feb. 12 – Driving on Interstate 15 in Littlefield, Arizona, with miles of road construction, just moving at 35 MPH.

Feb. 13 – In Fruita, Colorado, on I-70, I called my folks, while on my way East heading to and then through Vail Pass (10,662 feet elev.), which today is requiring chains. I can't yet do that. So, with approval from my DM (the C.R. England woman who is my Driver Manager), I shut down until roads cleared. I demanded that "If the old-time trucks are shut down, then so am I."

While in Fruita I plan to see "Dinosaur Journey Museum" across the street from where I'm holding. Amazing! Really cool stuff...dinosaurs are real...I've seen the proof.

In Colorado for the night. Chains are required on parts of highway 70. Clouds are coming...from the East. Looks like it's going to be a storm here tonight. So I'm staying put right here. I miss the snow...but not that much...giggles! I hope I miss the snow falling in tomorrow's drive.

Vail Pass highway (view on previous page) is 10,662 feet high mountain pass in the Rocky Mountains of central Colorado. I'm certainly seeing new and amazing scenes.

Six months ago, Loren West, a former long-haul trucker from Wisconsin, gave ABC News "20/20" a glimpse of what life is like behind the wheel of a big rig. Here is a portion.

"Graduating CDL (commercial driver's license) school and hiring on with a reputable company went well. It wasn't until I began my first run with a company trainer that the enormity of the challenge ahead set in. Traffic jams, blinding sun, freezing rain and road construction are conditions most commuters deal with on their way to work, but truckers deal with these obstacles (and many more) all day and every day as part of daily life. Multiply that times 18 wheels, 80,000 pounds, and a 70-foot rig, and it equates to a grueling way to earn a living.

Not long after the miles piled up and the wanderlust wore off, I concluded that truck driving is basically a factory job with a pleasant view. Long hours, low pay and constant deadlines are unavoidable. Couple that with endless government oversight, a lack of trucker-friendly facilities and being away from home for weeks at a time, and it creates what is termed among industry analysts as 'churn and burn.' It's a common saying among truckers that trucking isn't a job, or a career — it's a lifestyle. If that lifestyle continues to become even more difficult, keeping the safest and most dedicated drivers behind the wheel will be industry's biggest challenge."

Feb. 14 – Good news. So far it's just wet. But I didn't have to chain up....Snowy, slick, and windy...but I made it through. Safe and sound. On my way to Kansas, then back to Oakland. That evening: **Driving through Vail, Colorado.** Snowy, icy, windy. Going up and down, sharp turns too. Noticed car spinning-out facing the on-coming lane. I am careful; I drove 35 mph hazard light flashing too. It was scary.

What a screwed up day. Drove through snow, windy, icy roads. Key broke in the ignition, I get pulled over by the cops, my trailer lights weren't on, didn't get a ticket. I'm finally parked for the night, staying in Lamar in eastern Colorado at a truck stop.

Feb. 15 – Ulysses, Kansas, where President Grant is from. My, it's really windy here. Holding my steering wheel, as the tumbleweeds fly by on across the road. Late that Saturday: Liberal, Kansas where Dorothy from the "Wizard of Oz" is from - as I was driving through town. This is great...to get paid to travel like a tourist.

Trucking jokes are fun, if sometimes weird, off-color, nasty, poking fun at others, yet humorous. Here's one I just heard – probably an old one.

TWO TRUCKERS talking:-
Trucker 1: "Breaker breaker. I've got a pig stuck behind my bull bar. How can I get it out?"
Trucker 2: "Just slice the gut and let the insides drop out, then it'll fall straight down."
Trucker 1: "Thanks. Ten four." (a couple of minutes' silence)
Trucker 1: "Breaker breaker. OK, it's out, but now I've got another problem. What do I do with his motorcycle and helmet?"

Feb. 16 – Late morning on the I-40 near Paraje, New Mexico, a bit west of Albuquerque.

Mid-evening - In Kingman Arizona now for the night at a truck stop. Must be up tomorrow at 5 AM. and must deliver this load to the Port of Oakland by 7 AM on next Tuesday the 18th. I am keeping the prime meat I'm carrying at a steady 29 degrees F. (exactly -1.1 C.) to be shipped to Japan.

Feb. 18 – The meat load has been rescheduled for this morning. I dropped the load at a yard and another driver (with a TWIC card) picked it up. I already got another trailer from the yard where I dropped the meat load off. I'm staying in California for the next few days. Here is view of my very dirty truck cab and trailer. Time to fit in a truck wash stop.

I take this container and it will get live loaded in two places then dropped off in south California.

Most of my loads are full. I have had one run where I picked up two partial loads to take to one location.

Feb. 19 - I have one pick up at 1500 hours in San Leandro, then another at 2200 this evening in Gustine (east of San Luis Reservoir).

Feb. 20 - I should be dropping off my truck by Friday to start my few days off for "home time." Plus they can fix the ignition (as the key broke inside. Then I drop this load in Moreno Valley just east of Riverside at 0400. Late evening:- I'm at my drop off, but can't unload until 4 a.m., no bathroom, just watching movies on my big rig, last day of work.

Feb. 21 - My Friday finally came. I get a few days of home time, first day home...sleep, wash clothes, unpack and re-pack to get ready for my next 6 weeks.

I don't read truckers blogs. Most of the time I'm too tired and just go to sleep. However, recently my father sent me comments by "Trucker Mike" with the experience of several months. Recounting several stressful experiences with pre-plans, delivery logistics, parking, and bad directions, he wrote this which rings true in my experience of several months on the road:-.

"As terrible of a trip as this sounds, it was also a very rewarding one. I enjoy the challenge of these difficult situations. Many times I don't necessarily enjoy the stress as it's happening, but once it's over, I feel a great sense of satisfaction. And the tougher the situation, the more I learned from it .

"Truck driving can be filled with stress. I think I've learned how to deal with stress more in my time as a truck driver, than the rest of my life. If you're just getting into the industry, be aware that you will make some bonehead mistakes, you will require the help of others from time to time, and you'll wonder how you got into and out of certain situations. It just comes with the job, and everyone goes through it. The key is to take a deep breath, and deal with the situation at hand. As soon as you get into a hurry out here, is when people get hurt.

"Sometimes trips go very smoothly, and other times trips go like the one I just described. This is the reality of truck driving. Are you up for the challenge?"

--o-0-0-0-0--

One final thing. Thought I'd wind up this chapter with a few other facts about my truck. The fuel tanks are 100 gallons each and I have two of them one on each side. I have steer tires, one on each side. Two drive tires that are super singles on each side. On the chassis I have four duel tires on both sides. The steer tires are Michelin 275/80R22.5 x z a 3. Drive tires are super singles Michelin 445/50 R22.5 Tandem tires are Hi-way express 10.00-20. Or New Pride also 10.00-20.

An example of trucking complexity:- each state has its own weight limitations. A trip coast to coast crosses many states, and occasional weigh stations. Most containers are 40 feet long and will hold 19 pallets in a pinwheel pattern. I've seen smaller ones but I'm not sure their size. All containers on the chassis have a generator on the underneath of the container. The gauges are on the front of the container.

I have a fifth wheel (pictured on next page) that I back into a chassis to slide it on, and there is a kingpin on the chassis that slides on the fifth wheel and is latched around the kingpin. The sliding fifth wheel is so I can move the weight forward or back.

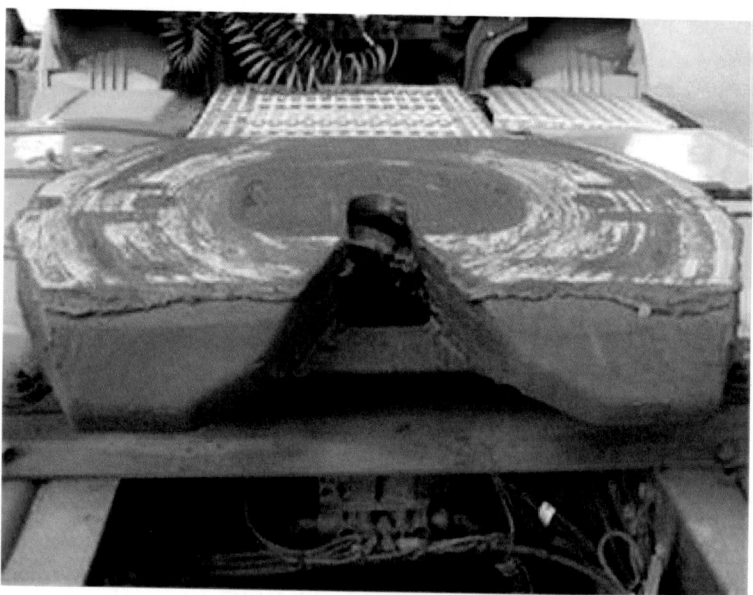

The chassis doesn't have a moving tandem like the fifty-three foot trailers does. So I don't have to move my tandems for the bridge law on containers. However, on a fifty-three foot trailer you can move them forward or backward, and yet they must be 40 feet from the kingpin to the first set of tandem axles.

Chapter 4:- The Trucker Rolls the Freight

Feb. 25, 2014 – Off on the next stage of my career as a long-haul trucker, still earning 27 cents a mile, now quite an experienced driver of a Freightliner "Cascade" 2012 truck, with the stock sleeper cab, a model with 72" high roof owned by C.R. England. And "my" Freightliner truck #59161 is in the CRE company's stock red color.

To provide some understanding of the remarkable standard features of this Freightliner Cascade, I insert this enumeration excerpted from its sales catalog:-

"Powerful HVAC system with 6 dash-mounted vents, 8 blower speeds and 20% greater airflow. High-tech thermal and noise insulation. Overhead storage console. Cab insulation and pre-stressed walls. Adjustable tilt-telescoping steering column. Low-mounted dash and sloped hood. Steering wheel mounted controls. Up to 50-degree wheel cut. EPA 2010-compliant SCR [Selective Catalytic Reduction] technology. Rugged three-piece bumper. Detachable three-piece rain tray and quick rear engine access. Gas strut-assisted hood. Roped-in windshield. And "Detroit Virtual Technician" integrated remote engine diagnostic system which records performance data immediately before, during and after a fault occurs."

Another 6 weeks on the road before another 4 days "home time," while averaging 500 miles a day. Home time was too short. Now I'm back to work, largely on a dedicated Western route. I'm now in Ontario, CA , picking up a load that is heading to Denver, Colorado.

Feb. 26, early afternoon – A problem, as I'm hardly out driving solo for more than one full day, there is something wrong with a tire. I pull over, get out and inspect, and find one has gone flat. So I'm limping in and getting it fixed in Las Vegas at the Southern Tire Mart, on Speedway Blvd. Welcome to trucking!

One inner tube blew when a screw got into the tube. I must have driven over the screw just in the right angle to get it stuck in the groove of the tread. Even with this inner tube problem, I will make my delivery a day early.

Later, at midnight, I report that I made it to Fruita, CO, after getting my tire fixed. Good night.

Feb. 27 - Driving through Colorado on the 70, now through Vail, snowing, icy roads. Notice I'm down-shifted for

down-hill grades and hazard lights are flashing. I'm doing great!

Feb. 28 - I'm back at Fruita CO. again, got my new load heading to Springfield, UT, so as to get a sticker for the truck, then I'm to drop the load in Carson CA. (Somehow I lost a day. I thought today was the 27th not the 28th of Feb.)

Mar. 1 – Via Vail, CO, and back into Utah in afternoon. Mar. 2, late evening:- Dropped load at Mira Loma yard after a 5 minute visit with Sharon and the kids to give them stuffed animals I bought at Dinosaur museum in Fruita, Colorado. Now going to sleep in Barstow at a truck wash. At a very quiet and safe place another driver told me about, at exit L. (I don't talk much with truckers for many are "creepy.") Good night all. I have to drive early morning to be in Utah to drop this trailer off.

Mar 3 – My DM finally got the message! Feeling much better...no stress on me. Deliver in the morning. I'm in Springfield, Utah. Shutting down for the night. Deliver in the morning, then go to the yard in Utah for stickers I need for the truck. Good night.

Mar 4 noon - No dock to pull up to. So they have to pull the pallets to the edge and use a forklift to bring it down. (Most of my loads are full; only one run where I picked up two partial loads to take to one location.) Now at Orem, UT, unloading travertine and natural stone products at Old World Stone Imports.

Mar 5, 10 pm – Visibility unsafe to drive further. I'm in Rock Springs, WY, on I-80, shutting down for the night. (There are so many snow fences in Wyoming, where it snows a lot, plus the wind gets to 50+ gusts there. That's why I was glad I had a heavy load to drive through there. If I had a light trailer, I would have to find another route to take. Thank goodness for snow fences!)

Still have 513 miles to go to Rocky Ford, CO. Good night.

39

Mar 6, via Ogden, Utah, and into Wyoming, where they have part of a fence... actually a snow fence so as to

influence drifting snow.

Mar 8, noon, at Wheat Ridge, Colorado, just NW of Denver on a warm day of 70. Then rain, then snow within minutes – Colorado weather to experience!!!

Now to have a lunch stop for servicing at a TravelCenters of America truck stop on I-70 at Exit 266. This nationwide firm (with 9 stops in California) here has truck parking with 163 spaces, restaurant, 7 showers, 2 truck service bays, 8 diesel dispensers, 1 diesel satellite pump, and the following other services for truckers:- truck scales, check cashing services, travel store, TripPak Express and Scanning, Interstate Speedzone WiFi, laundry room, driver's lounge, chiropractic services, Freightliner ServicePoint, preventive maintenance, standard services including tires and rapid oil change, StayFit Walking Trail, pet area, ministry services, Reserve-it Parking, J-Pro Diagnostics, service for HVAC and brake and electrical, Western Union, drug-testing service, and DAT load monitors, parking and showers for the handicapped, ATM, fax and copy service, as well as Department of Transportation inspections and physicals. TravelCenters of America (TA) is the largest full-service truck stop chain in North America, most common east of the Mississippi.

I listen to music on the road to pass the time of day. Early March, I asked my friends on Facebook "There are times when the world's asleep, the questions run so deep, for such a simple man... Can you name the artist?"

I've just heard and like a song by the popular English rock group Supertramp, recorded in 1970. I'll insert lyrics so you can read them, catching the inner mood, as it was put into a poem which expresses the universal wondering of a person feeling rather at a loss.

"*Logical Song*"

When I was young
It seemed that life was so wonderful
a miracle, oh it was beautiful, magical
and all the birds in the trees,
well, they'd be singing so happily
oh joyfully, oh playfully watching me.

But then they sent me away
to teach me how to be sensible
logical, oh responsible, practical
and they showed me a world
where I could be so dependable,
oh clinical, oh intellectual, cynical.

There are times when all the world's asleep.
The questions run too deep
for such a simple man.
Won't you please, please tell me what
we've learned. I know it sounds absurd,
but please tell me who I am

Now watch what you say
or they'll be calling you a radical,
a liberal, oh fanatical, criminal.
Oh won't you sign up your name?
We'd like to feel you're acceptable,
respectable, oh presentable, a vegetable!

At night when all the world's asleep,
the questions run too deep for such a simple man.
Won't you please, please tell me what
we've learned?
I know it sounds absurd but please tell me
who I am, who I am, who I am.

Keyboard player Roger Hodgson, who wrote this song and sang the lead vocals, said in a 2012 interview:

"I think it was very relevant when I wrote it, and actually I think it's even more relevant today. It's very basically saying that what they teach us in schools is all very fine, but what about what they don't teach us in schools that creates so much confusion in our being. I mean, they don't really prepare us for life in terms of teaching us who we are on the inside.

"They teach us how to function on the outside and to be very intellectual, but they don't tell us how to act with our intuition or our heart or really give us a real plausible explanation of what life's about. There's a huge hole in the education.

"I remember leaving school at 19, I was totally confused. That song really came out of my confusion, which came down to a basic question: please tell me who I am. I felt very lost. I had to educate myself in that way, and that's why California was very good for me to kind of re-educate myself, if you like."

Later Mar. 8, mid-evening - I thought I ran over a branch but the dragging sound didn't stop. So I pulled over and turned on four-way flashers and got out to look. Saw it was a flat. Sent a message to my company for road service. Looks like a nail hole that got my truck tire. I was in Roggen, Colorado, on the I-76 freeway at mile marker 49. Tire was still intact on the rim. No pulling to either side. Tire is off...new one to be put on...very soon. After that, to Nebraska, heading to Oakland, Iowa, pick up a load and head to California. Time to hammer down.

Mar 9 – Wrote my parents:- I got a container to the place before scheduled in the hours I had to drive. But I screwed up by taking an empty container and not a loaded one. I have not hit anything since I got on this container fleet (I'll explain "container" just below) ...so I expected to be yelled at or written up for this. I got to a truck stop, parked safely and legally, with permission from dispatch. So I will find out what they will do with me...I'm sure in the morning. Goodnight from Iowa. Your stupid daughter :-)

I shall now explain what happened:- I was given orders to pick up a container, but I read the numbers wrong and took an empty container to the drop off place. When I should have grabbed a loaded "Container" at the yard in Commerce City, Colorado. It was my fault for not checking all the numbers. I only looked at the first three numbers. Dyslexia doesn't make it easier...I normally would double check things...so I wouldn't screw it up. But it was cold, wet, and I had to hurry up and get the container rolling. Then I had the blow out with my tire. Driver Manager didn't know I had a blown tire when he was mad and sent me a message, that I only got 20 miles from the yard when I stopped. I had sent a message to road service not to my DM, driver manager. Once he found out I was stuck on the freeway I never heard from him.

Mar 10 - Everything is all right. I got new orders to pick up a load out here near Carnforth, Iowa, just 55 miles from the truck stop I'm at. My DM wasn't upset with me as I told her the truth. I just keep the container I have and take it to my pick up. Noon: Iowa on the 21 south going to Delta & Brooklyn. Then: I'm in Nebraska on the I-80.

Pictured here on top right-side dashboard is my mascot, a dinosaur from Fruita CO that I got from the dinosaur museum about a month ago. It is as close to a blue dragon as I can get at this time.

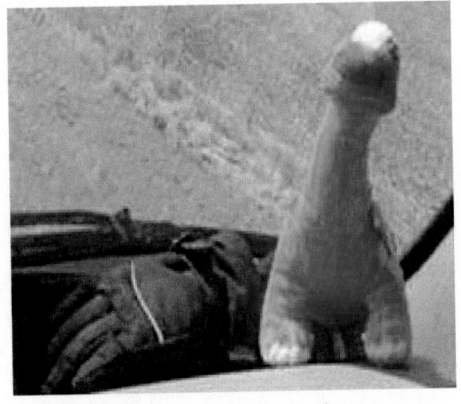

'Blue Dragon' is my c.b. 'handle' (a personal slang name used for Citizens Band Radio) which I've been called since

43

I was married to Larry, at the time when we worked on trucks way back then.

Mid-evening I'm at the Pilot Travel Centers' Truckstop in Camforth, IA, where the parking area was packed with truckers to sleep at night - Watching movies on my laptop, new load orders tomorrow morning. Phoned my parents, near midnight, to bring them up to date on activities of the road. I had dropped a container of a meat load off at Cargill, a famous very large company dealing in all sorts of agricultural commodities. I described the "container" as a very large metal box, 40' long and 12' wide, unitized, for ease in moving on and off oceanic transport ships. The container is placed on a chassis for trucking on land, with the refrigerator unit attached underneath – and very noisy.

Mar 11 - Been waiting here for 9 hours and still waiting for my loaded container to take to Oakland, CA.   I can't sleep, been trying all day, tossing and turning. It's not happening. It's a hurry up and get there ... now it's a waiting game, holding at Cargill Meat Solutions (in the beef, pork and turkey business), Wapello County

A grease fire in Cargill Meat Solutions' rendering department shot flames and black smoke into the sky Saturday afternoon. Photo provided by Tim Pouder.

Plant, Ottumwa, IA. This Cargill plant employees 2400 and has a daily hog kill of 18 to 19-thousand hogs. Two months ago this plant was evacuated following an ammonia leak. A year ago this month there was a major grease fire.

Mar 12, at 8 AM - I got my load last night, only had 2 hours of drive time left. The closest truck stop is 55 miles away but going east. The next one is 101 miles going west. It's raining and snowing.

So I asked the company if I could park here until after I got my loaded container (the right one). They say 'yes indeed' I could stay. It was better to stay here where I was around people, and not on the road, sliding on the road to a truck stop where I wouldn't have a parking spot as it was midnight. So I stayed put for the whole day and night.

An update at Noon:- Rain snow and windy last night. This morning clear skies and some wind... California here I come!

Mar 14, mid-evening - At 4-Way Bar Café & Casino restaurant, and then Petro Wells Truck Stop for the night, in Wells, Nevada, off the I-80 just west of Utah. Be in Sacramento tomorrow, then Oakland Monday morning.

Mar 15, mid-afternoon - In Spark's, Nevada, on the I-80 at T.A. #172 (with full name Travel Centers of America) walked from the truck stop to a wonderful restaurant "Cafe Bellini" with wonderful people and food. Should I stay here for the night? Leave AM for Sacramento?

Mar 16, mid-morning in Sacramento on the I-80, at 49er Travel Plaza (of the Pilot Travel Centers) – Lord, please get rid of this pounding headache I've had for weeks now. Will not leave until early morning, since this is closest place that is safe and close to Oakland for my drop.

Mar 17, at 4 AM - Good morning, I'm up, getting my cappuccino, then pre-trip inspection, then get those wheels rolling. Oh, and yes, I still have the head ache.

Mid-afternoon in Oakland:- I'm finally getting my fingers checked; x-ray proves that they are broken. But I had given myself great first aid; got a popsicle stick and taped the two fingers around the stick, which worked well.

I have medical insurance through my company, so that covered the cost. It happened then I was in southern California, about a month ago … silly me … I slammed the big rig door on my right hand middle and ring finger. I'm okay, just hard to shift gears and push in the air valves. Now tonight I'm back to Sacramento for a night.

Tomorrow at 1PM, I pick up a dry load in Fairfield, off the I-80, then in three days I shall reach Denver.

Mar 18 – My truck died in Emeryville on freeway 580 just after I picked up container from the Oakland yard. Alert indicator lights flashed red. Waiting on road service. It's crazy watching others crash. So far three accidents within a few minutes. People aren't watching what they are doing. Afternoon: Tow truck showed up. This is fun!!!

 Late evening of 18th: Let me see - truck broke down. Trailer was picked up by the company. The truck cab was hauled to a shop in Oakland, with me riding in tow truck and dropped at my hotel. It's going to take a few days before it's ready to roll. My phone dropped and cracked the phone screen. Cut my ring finger on left hand from picking up my phone after it dropped. Good news I'm in nearby Oakland's Days Inn (which the company is paying for), and a new phone will be delivered by Thursday...yeah!

WHAT HAPPENED? First was a light flashing on dashboard to alert to a problem, so I phoned C.R. England's Driver Manager and was told to push a button to rev up the engine so oil fluid would flow better. This fluid is the DEF (diesel exhaust fluid) which burns off at a specified temperature to reduce the exhaust pollution. The fluid was ¾ full, but it seems that the filter may have gotten clogged, causing another indicator light to come on and flash constantly. When another indicator light flashed red to indicate the truck must stop, the engine shut off in the middle of six lanes. I turned on emergency lights and carefully shifted lanes to get to side of the highway. I put out the mandated three triangular reflectors around the truck. (One was soon run over by an oncoming vehicle, and broken.) I called my Driver Manager, also for road service. She thinks I will be waiting for my truck repair which will take two or three days.

> DIAGNOSTIC? Early afternoon on March 20, Golden Gate Truck Center reported the following performed:- "Verified the Check engine light. Hooked up computer [and] found active codes for high soot levels. Followed troubleshooting steps, performed regen[eration]. Upon completion of successful regen DPF [Diesel Particulate Filter] zone now @ "0" (from [the initial] zone 5), rechecked that the [warning light] code is now inactive and there are no other codes. Performed short test drive, monitored DPF zone and found there are no other issues at this time. Prepared truck for customer pickup."

Until I had the repair report, I thought the DPF filter became clogged. From a manual one learns "DEF is stored in a tank on board the vehicle, and injected into the exhaust stream by a metering system. The injection rate depends on the specific after-treatment system, but is typically 2-6% of diesel consumption volume. This low dosing rate ensures long fluid refill intervals and minimizes the tank size (and subsequent obtrusion into vehicle packaging space). An electronic control unit adjusts the addition of fluid in accordance with such parameters as speed and engine operating temperature. Diesel engines can be run with a lean burn air-to-fuel ratio to ensure the full combustion of soot and to prevent the exhaust of unburnt fuel. The excess of oxygen necessarily leads to generation of nitrogen oxides which are harmful pollutants from the nitrogen in the air.

Selective catalytic reduction is used to reduce the amount of nitrogen oxides released into the atmosphere. Diesel exhaust fluid (from a separate DEF tank) is injected into the exhaust pipeline, the aqueous urea vaporizes and decomposes to form ammonia and carbon dioxide." In trucker's vernacular, the DEF fluid is horse and cow piss.

Mar. 20, evening in Fresno with my serviced truck – Got my truck back this morning. Picking up a "dry" load in

Fresno tomorrow morning, to take it to Denver.

Mar 21, mid-afternoon - Made my pick up early, so I was on time, but still waiting in Fresno to be loaded at Lyons Magnus, "A leader in the foodservice industry".

Mar 22, early morning - Got my truck washed, it's so clean! Staying here for the night in A & B Desert Truck Stop, Barstow, CA. Then to Vegas by tomorrow.

Mar 23, late evening - Dropped both containers. I'm done for the night...now to eat (as I haven't eaten all day, been very busy), then to sleep in Wheat Ridge, a western suburb of Denver, Colorado. Good night all!

Mar 25, late evening - Colorado to Kansas, then Kansas to Texas where parked for the night.

Mar 26 - I've been through sunny day, wind, sand storm, rain and snow all in one day. Went through New Mexico, and Arizona. I ran 636 miles in 10:36 hours. (First time over 630 miles!) Night in Kingman, AZ.

Mar 28 noon - Bus fire off to my right on I-80 in Oakland. Not a nice sight to witness.

Mar 29 near midnight - I was hit, on the 80 heading to Reno, on Donner Pass. Everyone is NOT hurt, no damage

to my truck or trailer. However, his SUV was damaged in his rear. He gave me his insurance info and then he left the scene. I called the police and made a report. I took this and 17 pictures of all conditions. This happened when the Toyota driver stupidly tried passing my truck by driving on the shoulder - without having any chains on!

There had been heavy wet snow for several hours, the highway patrol required chains on rear axle tires. The chains carried on my truck were not the correct ones, so had to wait six hours for a tow truck to come and put on correct chains - and pull my truck out of a foot of snow.

My load of wine is being taken via Nevada, Utah, and then through Wyoming to Colorado. It is due on Monday. But it will take me another day or two.

Mar 31 - Laramie WY for the night. Denver CO tomorrow morning. Here is a recent backing story:- GPS info is not always right! At Cortez, CO, on a one lane dirt road and ditch on both sides, I was using a GPS that got me lost and caused me to make a wrong turn into a dirt road. I found that out the hard way, having to back up since a cable guy in a van was stuck, blocking the whole road. With trailer fully loaded, I had to back up three miles on a dirt road!

April 2 - Good morning in Kearney, Nebraska. Hello Iowa later. That evening:- I just love how my company runs. They tell me to get an empty container, so I did. I drive all day to head to Iowa and I was in Nebraska almost to Lincoln when they call me and tell me I picked up the wrong container. So I'm not going to Iowa, with the container, I'm now going to Missouri. I get there and drop the container. I have to find a place to shut down for the night, with 4 minutes to get to a fuel stop found a fuel station that has trucks here, I made it.

April 3 in evening - When they tell me to pick up an empty I will pick up a K-Line. If they wanted me to pick up a different container, they let me know the unit number. So I did what I was asked...get an empty. Next time I should make them tell me the unit number for any container. This was NOT my fault on this one. It was fun driving through fog rain on two lane roads all day long through Colorado, Nebraska, Kansas, then Missouri. It's foggy weather on the 29 N...in Missouri. Good night all.

April 4 early morning - Picked up a load yesterday from Milan, Missouri. Enjoyed some yummy Indian food. Spent the night in York, Nebraska, with heavy winds!

April 5 - Good morning, early start Wyoming to Utah, maybe Nevada, then California. I hope I have enough rollover hours to make this run. I need a 34 hour restart (rest period). Early next morning:- Good morning, it's time for me to get up and drive for 5:13 hours, then rest for 10 hours then drive 7:53 hours. I REALLY need to take a 34 hour restart so I can run. It's what I'm allowed to drive. Running out of hours. Law says I can only drive 11 hours in a 14 hour day. Landed in Wells, NV.

My snapshot above: Mad at Prest trucker (out of Indiana) leaving his truck blocking the fuel line in Cheyenne WY.

April 6, Sunday:- Rain then snow. Dang it! I don't get to drive today. Stuck in Imlay, Nevada, (population of 171 people) at a truck stop on the I-80. I ran out of hours. I gain 8 hours tomorrow, right after midnight.

I'm forbidden by law to drive more hours – until midnight when I could legally drive again. I called by DM, explained why I'm stuck, that I routinely sleep during the night so I should not drive after midnight tonight for it would be dangerous, so I can't deliver the load to Oakland tomorrow by 7 a.m., probably not until 2:30 or 3 Monday afternoon.

April 7 - I have a website on Facebook that I help run, called "American Truckers Online" which is described as: "Life of the American Truck Driver on the road. Bringing you the adventures and drama that we face each and every day. My hope for this page is to share photos both good and bad of accidents, corruptions, and dignity for 'The American Trucker,' heavy duty trucks that we American truck drivers see and use every day."

And early this evening:- Dinner for one please. I'm on my 34 hour restart. Rented a car to go home to Arroyo Grande, to get my tax papers sent off. On the way I stopped for dinner at Outback Steakhouse in Salinas.

April 9, early evening - I get to go home now...not on the 15. Plus I get 4 days off...yeah! I have to do work at my place, no fun. The Oak Tree apartment above mine sprang a water leak couple of days ago, damaging my place. But I will have help, as I paid for my ex-husband to pack my things and put them in storage for me.

(I'm at wheel in photo I uploaded after a truck wash.)

April 13, Sunday:- Raising the roof in God's house — at Five Cities Vineyard Church.

April 16:- Drove to Los Vegas last evening. Now I'm on the road heading to Denver. In evening:- I am now in Fruita, CO, for the night. Deliver by tomorrow in Denver. Heard from a classmate of mine, that of 150 in my driving class, 149 left because of the pay or for health issues. I'm the only one left still working for C.R. England.

April 17-18:- I left Colorado this morning, got to Kansas, dropped my empty container and picked up a loaded container of meat. Went to bed with a swollen left ankle, woke up to it throbbing. I must have stepped on it wrong yesterday. Thank God, it's only my clutch foot, not my fuel and brake foot. I'm now bedding down in Oklahoma. The scenery through the West is awesome. Highway I-40 is particularly nice with rolling fields, mountains, grand skies with impressive clouds.

On the next page I insert another photo to give you more of the "feel" of the western scenery.

April 19:- Well, I made it to Gallup, NM, safe and sound. There was fuel on the bottom of my shoe and when I stepped down I fell down on my butt, twisted my ankle. I told my DM so they know I'm hurt but going to see if I can still run this load to Oakland.

Gallup for the night. Foot on ice and it's raining ... watching a movie; must sleep so as to drive in the wee morning. Good night all.

April 21:- I drove 5 hours yesterday, Sunday. As my ankle started throbbing once again, I put ice on it and fell asleep. DM changed my delivery to Tuesday, tomorrow morning.

Also, I got a three-cent raise – a 10% increase, from 27 cents per mile to 30 cents - based on the monthly company requirement to watch safety videos and answer questions.

April 22 – I delivered my load. Now picking up my TWIC and TSA cards, so I now can go to major US ports. TWIC (shown on next page) was paid for by the company at cost of $129. The TSA was paid by me at $86.

My ankle is much better. Knee is throbbing from heavy traffic this morning. Cleaned truck and windshield, ate dinner. Movie time.

TI have no new orders so I'm at a truck stop for the night. I had to pick up a chassis and take it to a place where they put

a container on it. Then I used zip ties to keep the handles in place so the container doesn't come off the chassis. It hasn't been a good driving day because there was no load leaving Oakland. I only drove 100 miles to a truck stop that is the closest to Oakland. At this time, I don't know where I will be going to next.

April 23, noon:- Still at the Petro truck stop in Los Banos, just off I-5 east of San Luis Reservoir, no new orders, just an empty container...movie time. I have been down before for two days. It's called a restart or reset of hours. I always seem to keep moving, so this unexpected down time is a bit bothersome. Ankle is much better, no problems walking at all. I've been watching an actor called Jackie Chan who is funny and I like martial arts. Mid-afternoon: I go tomorrow to Napa and American River canyon for pickups, then head to Denver.

April 24, mid-evening:- I'm in Sparks, NV. Got two loads of wine on this container. I was given soup by friend; had enough money for toast as I still have salad on my truck from lunch. I have money for breakfast in the morning, just trying to budget my food intake so I don't become a fat trucker. I get paid from work on Tuesday, $378.00, but I live on $100.00 a week. So I can save money for something I need. Not for what I want.

April 25, early afternoon:- Just passed Wells, NV. Rain dancing on my windshield to the music, thanks to Rain-X (Rain-X is a wax to put on your windshield so the rain and snow float away.) My radio is a Series XM so I can listen to music. While it's raining in Nevada, the rain is dancing on my windshield, with the beat of music from my XM.

April 26, very early morning at C.R. England headquarters in West Valley City, outside of Salt Lake City:- I've got to get moving, but there is still winter warnings in April! Snow, gusts of winds, through Wyoming and parts of Colorado and I have to deliver in Denver. Stopped in Little America Travel Plaza on I-80, Wyoming, to drop mail off and eat. I hope the rest of the day isn't bad, as I heard it was going to be snowing in Laramie and Cheyenne Wyoming. It's been raining all morning. Later:- I made it to Denver, CO, for the night. Doing a local delivery in the morning here.

April 27 - Eight cars flipped over on the I-76 between mile markers 100/120, everyone dead, in the 33 miles between Brush and Sterling, CO, due to heavy winds and rain.

April 28, mid-afternoon - Made it! I don't know what I'm hauling, for this load only has numbers. Holding early afternoon at the Loves Truck Stop on I-90 Sioux Falls, South Dakota. Less than 5 miles for load delivery in the morning. By 10 this evening another driver will meet me here and swap containers, then he will make my delivery in the morning here. I'm taking his 243 miles to Fargo, ND, by tomorrow morning so I will be driving at night.

April 29 – I tried to sleep but was unsuccessful. So I drove at 1:00 a.m. and got here at 6 a.m. I'm beat! (Posted several dawn pictures today on Facebook for my friends.) Made my Fargo, ND, drop of wine cases on time. — I am here at the Republic National Distribution, the #2 US distributor of premium wine and spirits.

Chapter 5 – My Life Driving for C.R. England

April 29, 2014, this evening I wrote my folks: -"Thank you father and mother for the gift after one full year [from when I started truck driving school].

It will be one year on October 17th that I've worked as a truck driver with my United States Commercial Driver's License – and was hired. Indeed my journey started a year ago from today.

" It's been an adventure. *I love this job.*"

April 30 - Via Owatonna, Minnesota, off the 35 south. Heading to Marshalltown, IA, to pick up a loaded container after dropping my empty there. Then heading to Oakland.

Late evening:- I nearly get hit by a swerving truck and trailer on the freeway. Did a washout of the container and then I dropped my clean empty container in Marshalltown, and picked up a loaded container at the same location.

I don't have any more DOT drive time available - so I can't drive longer. Therefore I'm staying in Marshalltown, IA. Good night all. It's been a crazy day.

May 3, 2014 – On I-80 in West Wendover, Nevada, truckers can stop at the Truckers Lounge with a Class-A license, get free showers and coffee, also get trucker's discount coupons for the greatest buffet the Mongolian BBQ at the Rainbow Hotel Casino. They also give you coupons for Rainbow Casino, or the Peppermill Casino. Spending tonight in Winnemucca, heading west.

(There was no location in Facebook to tell where the Truckers Lounge is, so I took this picture – and Facebook is now using my picture at West Wendover.)

There's an interesting online Website called "TruckingTruth Blog" with several dozen of informative articles about "truck driving lifestyle," including articles by three women truckers. There are several online blog sites, some good, some interesting, some primarily complaining -- which suggests the character of people who take up the big-rig trucking career life.

May 4, 2014 - I phoned Dad about 3pm Sunday the 4th from Sacramento, telling him I expect to make my first Port of Oakland delivery to a container ship heading across the Pacific - scheduled for mid-afternoon. My delivery is now legal since I have my TWIC - the Transportation Worker Identification Credential (a federal government ID that all port workers and truckers need, required when working in a port receiving or sending shipments abroad). I was lucky(?) and didn't have to go to Port today. It was closed.

Well, dropped my container and tried to hook up two different chassis, neither would move. Brake chamber was locked up on the chassis so I couldn't move it. (I found out how to unlock it the next morning. I push in the truck brake valve and leave the trailer valve pulled out for 5 minutes and air builds up in chassis.)

I was given new orders by my DM Terra to pick up a loaded container; she's always very understanding and helpful. (We drivers are not allowed to meet any DM, since an irate driver some time ago came and attacked a DM. Thus all DMs are off limits.) This new load is heading east, so I'm back to Denver.

This is one of the examples why the DM is important for proper managing the C.R. England trucks and drivers, for delivery or pickup problems are frequent, schedules have to change with weather or road conditions, mechanical problems. And a strike can close for hours or days the Port or other destination. The logistics of long-haul trucking present constant challenges to all concerned. I'm still learning ... every day.

Tonight I'm in Sacramento at the 49er Travel Plaza, since I didn't have enough hours to make it to Reno. Beautiful fields so often along the roads in the San Joaquin Valley of California.

Here is part of Karen Smith's blog "Blessings and Gifts" -- which echoes my thoughts.

In all my travels I've noticed quite a few different things, but the thing that mystifies me the most is the "magic" of just being....Observing the trees as they sway in the breeze, in accordance with natures actions, like a symphony of music with all the right instruments playing all the right notes for perfect harmony. As we drive the highway, we come across a cottonwood tree looking so out of place in the dessert, next to the road and standing so tall as if to tell everyone going by that it can survive in any type of setting and surroundings...to become adaptable.

59

This load is to be in Denver May 6th at 8 a.m. They are going to have to change the appointment, have me swap with driver that has a team to run it there on time.

May 5, 2014 - FOOD!!! Made it here for the night. YEAH!!! — back in familiar West Wendover, Nevada, nearly at Utah border.

May 6 at dawn - Can I go back to sleep for an hour? No, darn it. It's okay, I've been up. Time to get rolling. I'm leaving W. Wendover, NV.

Where do you think I can get to at 50 mph in 8.45 hours of driving? Anyone going to guess?

I just saw a truck with his double flipped over. Winds over 65 mph took this one. A road service truck now there to help. Took picture, posted it at "American Trucker Online."

I feel the wind sharply pushing my trailer and cab. Well, mid-afternoon, I have run out of driving time on the I-80 in Rock Springs, middle of Wyoming, at the Flying J with its much smaller truck parking. Only got to drive 6 hours today, with four hours scheduled for tomorrow. Denver has to wait while I'm resting. Good night all.

May 7 – Good morning, as it's hailing this morning in Rock Springs. Icy fog, and rain, and hail, and snow, then back to

just overcast. Made it here to Cheyenne, at the Flying J. I only had 5 hours and 44 minutes of drive time allowed today. If only I had 2 more hours I'd have delivered today. Evening at the Flying J. with heavy rain, thunder and lightning.

My friend Brenda tells me "Just remember. Thunder is the sound of God bowling. Lightening is two ways.....big bright flashes means he got a strike, and lesser bright means he got a spare." I like the way you think on that...giggles. Brenda: "How do you think I got myself and my kids to not be afraid." I told her I love the idea...it calmed me down. Thanks girlie :-)

Only have 92 miles to make my drop in Denver tomorrow! Predicting "strong storms" and snow tonight! Good night all. Altogether, quite a day of weather! Reminds me of the final of Karen Smith's blog:-

I'm finding out that beyond the stressful factors of this career I can also be able to become part of what's been created as a gift to relish within my soul. Finding out that life is a spiritual experience to be replicated from one to another. Being in a truck...nothing else can compare to the unity that's created and felt from me to my Creator ~ God!!!

As I work this business, I learn of trucking companies' ethical practices, quality of management, and business and financial processes. Interesting to read online about this skeptically during my off-work time, sometimes before dropping off to sleep.

Here, a few years old, are unedited samples at the 'Truckers Report.' Firms are only listed if they have serious problems with drivers.

Firm E [does] not pay their lease operators properly; drivers have stated that they will rip you off.
Firm H does NOT pay drivers layover for sitting on weekends. If their drivers sit all 48 hours on the weekend away from his/her family, they don't get a dime.
Firm S many drivers say they have cheated them, ran shoddy equipment, blatantly told drivers to lie on logs, not reimbursed tolls, etc. And recently has turned their trucks up to 65 mph to try and plug the hemorrhage of drivers leaving the company.
Firm T makes drivers falsify logs and violate hours of service rules. These drivers have also reported them to the DOT which has apparently done nothing. Drivers state that they have them recorded on tape, telling them to run illegal. Driver was fired, as the boss caught him recording the illegal directives.

I realize that there often is another side to complaints. A problem over some months may be corrected and not reported. And personnel problems can lead to complaints, and later corrected. Relationships can become frayed, as it can be in any line of competitive business, even in the non-profit sector - as my father has told me about working in a large university setting.

This evening I watched Big Rig Video and saw dozens of

cool trucks. Some awesome interiors.

On the next page, have a gander inside Rabbit River II Transport's 359 called "Gold Digger," shown at this 75 Chrome Shop Truck Show. I looked over 60 trucks of all kinds assembled for this huge show near Orlando Florida. This sure is a COOL A$$ truck...where can I get one?

May 8 - Here I come Dorothy (in the "Wizard of OZ"), to Liberal, Kansas. Aha! Here is the snow! Good night all...it's a chilling night here in Cheyenne WY.

Driving today, I had storm in Hugo, Colorado, and then sun in Kit Carson, Colorado, with the storm behind me. Saw lightning that lit up the WHOLE sky...it was amazing! No thunder yet...maybe later on tonight.

Well, it is evening and dark. I'm going to eat, watch a movie, then count some sheep ... giggles ... Nighty nite all, heading southeast at Liberal, Kansas, by the Oklahoma State line.

May 9 – This morning I delivered an empty dry container to National Beef, in Liberal Kansas. Then I picked up a loaded container of meat to take through Kansas, Oklahoma, Texas, New Mexico, Arizona, then back to California -- back for drop-off in Oakland.

In eastern New Mexico, I passed an interesting monument at Tucumcari on US 54. The scenery is marvelous and the old Apache legend is *very* interesting.

Evening:- I could only make it from Liberal, KS, to Grants, NM, well west of Albuquerque on highway I-40, which is my favorite highway due to its up and down mountains – lovely scenery.

May 10 – This morning on I-40 drove near the Petrified Forest National Park. Later, hub seal on chassis is leaking. Truck is making a buzzing sound when I go up hill and when I accelerate. Mid-evening at Petro Truck Stop in Kingman, AZ, and got the hub seal fixed. But they couldn't fix the buzzing sound. Have to take truck to dealership in the morning to have it looked at.

May 11 - Dealership won't look at it until tomorrow. Got a room for night at Knights Inn. My 2012 Freightliner Cascadia has 270,061 miles on it now; when I got the truck it had 226,242 miles. So in 12 months I've driven it 44,000 miles through much of the western states.

May 12 - Well, my truck is in the shop. I took the mechanic out for a test drive to let him hear the sound. It's more of a squeal then a buzzing sound. It happens only when driving, when I accelerate. So I think it could be a pinch in the fuel line. But I will wait to find out for sure what it is. Very puzzling!

Later, mid-afternoon, truck is fixed at Great West Truck Center across from the County Fair Grounds in Kingman, Arizona. It was a $1.76 clamp that was broken. Under warranty, so I'm ready to roll again.

Later:- Yes, it was on the fuel line, just like I thought. Tonight I'm in C.R. England's Mira Loma yard.

May 13 - I visited Sharon and the kids this afternoon, now I'm with Natalie and Liberty and the kids. Showed them the "In-Cab Navigation" system on my dashboard. I insert in the next page a picture which shows what it looks like, though it's actually much larger in the cab.

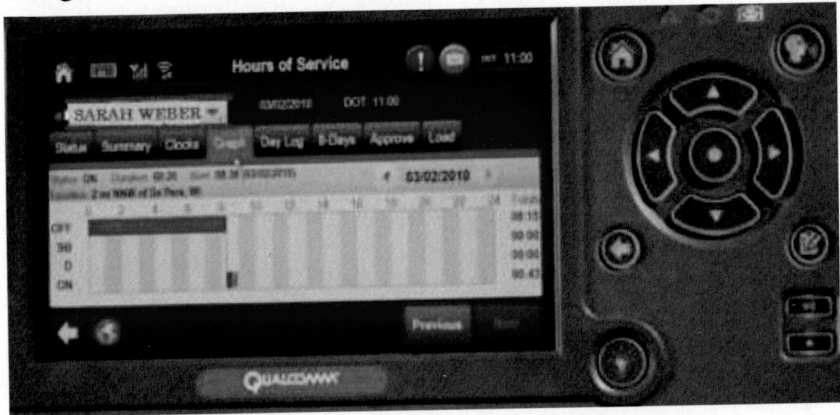

This great technology is described as constantly giving "accurate, up-to-date, interactive maps, dynamic truck routing, and turn-by-turn directions. A great asset as a mobile information system for trucking fleets. Automatic avoidance of truck-restricted routes for customizable vehicle profiles." It sends and receives messages, and records all that I do with this truck.

Ready to roll again. I picked up an empty container, goes to Colorado on 14th, where, in Fruita, I have a visit to the Dinosaur Journey Museum, where saw this.

What a treat to see all the dinosaurs on display!

May 15 - From sunshine, rain, to snow flurries driving about 35 mph up the west side of the Rocky Mountains to truck stop in Wheat Ridge, CO. Deliver in morning.

About 50 miles west of Denver, I drove once again to the Eisenhower- Johnson Tunnels running 1.7 miles under Continental Divide on the I-70 at 11,000 foot elevation (with two-lanes each direction) -- quite an experience when driving through it on the 1.64% grade. (here below is the tunnel approach I took while driving from the west side.)

"Due to additional height restrictions from variable message signs and lighting systems, the original clearance of the tunnels was 13.5 feet (4.1 m). The trucking industry lobbied to increase the vertical clearance of the tunnel. With a 2007 retrofit that used lower profile lighting and signs, it is now possible for trucks 13.92 feet (4.24 m) to navigate the tunnel, an increase of 5 inches (13 cm) over the original limit. Sensors will activate audible sirens near each entrance of the tunnel if a vehicle above the posted height attempts to enter the tunnel. Traffic signals at that entrance will turn red, stopping all traffic."

May 16 – Heading back west. I phoned my mother to consult about where and how to have a dentist fix a tooth cap which fell off, tooth now hurting inside of mouth.

May 17 - I haul wine east and meat to the west. Going straight to Oakland, CA. For the night in Wendover, Utah, at the Nevada border. Free showers for truckers at Truckers Lounge here.

May 18 - I talked to a different dentist to see who will put the tooth back in for $50.00. He was Twisten's dentist. I will see him when I arrive into Mira Loma.

Found out our company is moving from Mira Loma to Colton on May 23rd this year, so I have until June 15th to move my car. England moves its lot 20 miles, from west of Riverside to a lot off the I-10 north of Riverside.

When parked in Wendover NV, I see that I have a blown chassis tire. The company is sending someone to fix the tire. I was up waiting all day, lost six hours of drive time waiting for the tire repair man to show up. Turns out the tire had dry rotted which is rare, quite unusual. Took this picture below to show the damage.

The truck came and the guy took the old tire off, put the new tire on, and I was rolling again. I drove until I was tired and made it to the Petro Truck Stop in Sparks, NV for the night.

May 19 – Today I must deliver to Oakland before 3pm. Late afternoon, made my drop, now waiting for new orders.

I just found out my loan for C.R. England will be paid in full by July 20, 2014 -- as long as I stay working for this company until then. *Yeah!*

There are weekly safety meetings to attend, watch video and answer questions each month or I lose a half a penny per mile for a month. I was a team driver for three weeks, and, when I kicked out my team driver and drove on my own, I got 27¢ per mile. The longer you stay, the more pennies you can make. If you team up or become a trainer, you get 30¢ per mile on the truck miles – truck miles, not driver miles. When and if I do go to international ports, I get $30.00 more on top of 30¢ per mile.

May 20 - No new orders. Relaxing. in Santa Nella at the TA off the I-5 east of Pacheco Pass. Been here last night. Looks like I'm doing a 34-hour restart - meaning I will gain more drive hours. Better than having to drive 4 hours here, 6 hours there, and 9 hours after I have a load.

May 21, after 37 hours waiting, I now have a full 70 hours to run for the next 8 days.

Best news is that on July 20th my loan will be paid in full. Then I can leave CRE for a different company to drive for, one that will give me two weeks out on the road and then two days home so I can check my mail, make doctor appointments, as I will be running with Twisten. I'm filling out the application for it right now.

In a few minutes I will have to do my safety call and listen to questions that other drivers have.... Safety meeting was short ... all done. Off to get my load to pick up sparkling cider at Martinelli's in Watsonville, CA. Then three drops, two in Utah and one in Denver. By June 10th I should have "home time."

May 22 – Brought load to Sparks, Nevada, to spend the night. Dust storm here, blowing me down. Thank God I'm not having to drive any more tonight. On to Utah.

May 23, late afternoon - Food!!! French dip and cottage cheese, at Rainbow Hotel Casino in West Wendover, near the Utah border. Then, late evening, arrived at Salt Lake City hdqtrs of C.R. England. Looks like a weekend here...ugh... this load may not be delivered until the 27th. Since I always say "Heavens to Betsy," Twisten gave me a teddy bear which I named "Ta-Betsy" –all dressed up, in its first portrait.

May 24, early afternoon - Well, got to drop my container at the yard in Salt Lake City. Got new orders to pick up another container that goes to Oakland, but the crank-down landing gear is stripped, thus I'm waiting on the shop to fix it. Later, landing gear fixed and I'm rolling.

Late evening: Made it in the nick of time to Fernley, Nevada, I-80 just east of Reno. Get a bite to eat, then sleep time, for me. Good night all.

-- P.S. I'll add a postscript to explain the "nick of time." The US Department of Transportation (DOT) regulates the number of hours that a truck driver may drive per day as well as the total number of hours he/she may work per day and per week.

All of the next page are selected Federal rules for multi-day (long distance) trucking schedules.

Drivers may drive up to 11 hours, but are limited to 14 hours in a duty period

Drivers must take a mandatory 30 minutes break by their eighth hour of coming on duty

The 14-hour duty period may not be extended with off-duty time for breaks, meal and fuel stops, etc.

Drivers can restart the 7-day period once per every 168 hour work week, by taking at least 34 consecutive hour's off-duty with two consecutive periods of 1:00 a.m. to 5:00 a.m.
*The work week starts after the last legal reset. For example, if you begin at 1:00 a.m. on Monday, then your 168 work week continues until 1:00 a.m. on the following Monday. If you start at 12:00 a.m. the following Monday, you will have to run on the 60/7 rule as you will not have received a legal reset.

Each duty period must begin with at least 10 hours off-duty

Drivers may work 60 hours on-duty in seven consecutive days

On-duty time does not include any time resting in a parked vehicle (also applies to passenger-carrying drivers). In a moving property-carrying CMV, does not include up to 2 hours in passenger seat immediately before or after 8 consecutive hours in sleeper-berth.

If a driver cannot safely complete the run within the maximum driving time of 11-hours, that driver may drive up to an additional two hours in order to reach a place offering safety for the driver and cargo. However, the driver may not drive after the 14th hour since coming on duty.

If weather conditions will not safely allow you to pull off (i.e. at a hotel, truck stop, etc.) and stop for 10 hours off-duty, then you may extend your drive time up to two hours

This exception does not mean that you can work longer because of bad weather. If you can safely stop and layover within your 11 hour drive time you must do so (provided you cannot make it back to your home terminal within 14 hours, or under the 16-hour exception, if available.

Any period of 34-consecutive hours off-duty will restart the 60/70 hour calculation The restart must include two periods of 1:00 a.m. to 5:00 p.m.   Drivers may only use the 34-hour restart once per 168 hour week.

--o-o-o-o-o--

May 25 –Morning run from Fernley to Sparks for lunch. Midafternoon reached Sacramento 49er Travel Plaza with temperature 94-100, for sunbathing! My delivery early tomorrow is at the Port of Oakland. Gate opens up at 7 a.m. it's 84 miles from Sacramento. I should get up by 4:30 grab my coffee and pre-trip the truck and container and then I get rolling no later than 5 a.m.

May 26 - I hate it when I can't sleep, when I really need to. About 5 a.m., I wish I were a man right now so I could go for a walk. But if I do now, the truckers will think I'm a lot lizard. It's scary at times rolling into a truck stop getting hit on by another trucker.

Dang this day is going great! My pre-trip found three back lights out and a chassis tire flat due to valve stem. I'm at the 49er Plaza, and they don't work on the split rims ... waiting on roadside service. Load will be late.

At 7 a.m., the pictured valve stem melted on the rim that flattened my tire. The 49er wouldn't do the work, so another person did. The 49er Plaza doesn't take care of women drivers; they wouldn't serve me this morning even in the restaurant.

At 11 am, I'm in the Port of Oakland now. Showed my TWIC license, got new Good Trouble code from my DM, received tracking card to use while inside the Port, had truck weighed, drove through a maze of containers, had crane lift my meat load off (going to Japan), and I'm out of

71

the Port in 30 minutes! No typical long line of half a mile waiting, probably because today is Memorial Day.

Mid-afternoon I'm back to 49er Travel Plaza in Sacramento and its high temperature. Only five hours driving today. Loading wine in two places tomorrow, then heading to Denver via the I-80. (I've been told that the 70 is closed due to a land slide 8 miles long from my favorite trucker.)

May 27 – In Sparks, Nevada. I'm listening to symphony pops on my XM radio -- was playing Strauss and now Gershwin's "An American in Paris" one of my favorites. Twisten has told me to listen to something calming while driving in storms to keep me calm. I'm shutting down here for the night, with my blue dinosaur mascot.

May 28 - West bound on I-80, in Wells, NV, a huge truck and trailer turned over. It is sad to see. But I'm still proud to be a good safe driver, driving in my comfort zone. Mid-evening at TA Travel Center, out on west side of Salt Lake City, Utah. Good night all.

May 29 – Baked salmon, with cottage cheese and peaches - that's what's for dinner!!! Tonight at Johnson's Corner Truck Stop on the I-25 in Johnston, CO, heading south to Denver.

May 30 at 8 a.m. - I've never experienced this, so much trouble just to deliver a load. If late, then I have to get authorized money to pay the receiver. Now the receiver told me that they don't take deliveries after 8 a.m., and I have to have my company reschedule this load. But authorization for the "comchek" is still not valid...ugh! (Comchek is a fuel and cash card for the trucking industry.)

I'm at United Natural Foods in Aurora, CO, delivering load of oil and vinegar. (UNFI is a major wholesale distributors of natural, organic, and specialty foods with 25 distribution centers that supply 65,000-plus items.) I have been here once before when they tried to charge me a late fee of $150.00.

My DM had to call them and straighten things out, and I didn't have to pay anything as I wasn't late. Twice I've had problems here. Today I had to write a comchek for $53.00 as, due to DOT driving hour limitations, I was late one hour (7 am arrival instead of 6 am).

Again, DM (Driver Manager) called the company so now I'm being unloaded. I'll add that company delivery docks commonly schedule delivery times to keep personnel and dock space efficiently used.

There are industry- standard fees on a sliding scale for missing scheduled times, 1) late fee, 2) lumper fee (for "lumper" men who off-load and load), and 3) pallet fees (since pallets are heavier than loading on "slip sheets").

Late evening, ran out of hours for the day, so shutdown at the Chuckwagon Restaurant and Fastlane #20 Truckstop in Liberal, Kansas, to drop shipment early tomorrow.

May 31 – The trucks I see on the highways are Allied, Clark, Crete, CRST, C.R. England, J.B. Hunt, Knight, KTS, Marten, Prime, Swift, Schneider, United, U.S. Express, Werner, Xtra, to name those I mostly see on the road.

Very often it is fellow drivers I see in C.R. England trucks. The trucking industry is *huge*. A few companies like UPS are publically held. Some specialize in LTL, meaning the shipment is less than a total load.

Of the op carriers by some criteria, C.R. England is the 8th largest, doing $1,258 billion in 2013 revenue – a 9.8% growth. Looks like we are the largest privately-held firm handling "dedicated" work on a national basis, and also strong in the refrigerated chilled and frozen market.

C.R. England is among the top in its business, for the type of long-haul which I like to handle, and enabling me to have my home in California and often see my family.

RANK	CARRIER NAME	2011 REVENUE ($MILLION)
1	Swift Transportation	$3,021
2	Schneider National	$2,600
3	Werner Enterprises	$1,684
4	Landstar System*	$1,660
5	U.S. Xpress Enterprises	$1,570
6	J.B. Hunt Transport Services	$1,536
7	Prime**	$1,206
9	C.R. England	$1,007
8	Crete Carrier Corp.	$942
10	Greatwide Logistics*	$907

Another interstate trucking company is Temp Trans LLC, based in Adelanto, California. This company hauls fresh produce, chemicals, paper products, refrigerated food, beverages, and general freight using 18 trucks with 29 drivers, and last year logging 3,954,944 miles.

Rolling on my favorite highway I-40, while I am enjoying symphony music. (I-40 runs from Barstow to North Carolina, with some great scenery, good pavement, no construction, no traffic jams, good services.) I'll be stopping tonight in Jamestown, east of Gallup, out of DOT time, hauling a loaded container of meat going to the Port of Oakland.

My friend Twisten has worked for Temp Trans LLC with satisfaction; he explains to me that this company and its routes enable California drivers to be home weekends, be paid each week, earning 42¢ a mile (which can result in each team driver making as much as $1,500/week). With this type schedule, Twisten has less stress and more control over all aspects of his life.

June 1 at 3:30 – I phoned my father to report that in western-most Arizona on I-40 I saw a van heading east drive off the road, dust flying around, bodies on the ground, windshield broken, car parts scattered, traffic heading east stopped immediately. Dreadful sight.

I drive on into CA. At A&B Truck Stop in Barstow, got my truck washed for $30.00 and "every Sunday a free BBQ for anyone that shows up." Good night all.

There are risks in life, including a life as a trucker. It can be scary out here. That's why I post when I can. My parents know my truck is # 59161 as do my kids.

I never liked reality shows since they show you bad things that are happening, which gives high ratings on shows.

I do what I can to protect myself from situations that can get me into a bad way. I carry a Tazer to shock whoever steps up behind me or tries to hurt me in any way. I stay in my truck as much as possible and have it locked at all times, park near other drivers so, just in case I scream, trusting that someone, if needed, will call the police and/or come to my rescue.

A website I saw shows what I have had to experience. All what they said, I've dealt with. Then I think it over. It's rough some times, but ultimately I feel like I get paid to take a long vacation.

June 2 – Today the schedule has me driving straight from Barstow on 58, through Mojave, over the Tehachapi Pass, and picking up 99 at Bakersfield, then shortly jogging west on 46 to the I -5, and all the way up to the 580 which will take me through Livermore and into the Bay Area to Oakland.

Noon, received word from my DM. Rescheduled delivery to Oakland for tomorrow 7 AM, as I expected. Now I must pay for Internet service for my laptop so I can update my Rand McNally GPS. Right now my engine's running to keep me cool since it is 90° and very windy here. Truck is blowing side to side like a sailboat on the ocean. Staying the night on I-5 at Santa Nella Travel Center near San Luis Reservoir.

June 3 - I have two weigh stations before I get to Port tomorrow. One is 5 miles ahead of me on the I-5, the other is on the 580. June 3-5, all weigh stations are fully armed, with officers checking every 3rd truck for illegal and safety issues, a procedure which is conducted during a 72-hours period, once every year. Here on next page is approach to

Sacramento weigh station. I was inspected and weighed in Lane C.

May 26th I made my first delivery to the Port of Oakland. The massive size and activity, and the sheer complexity of the Port is shown by photographs found online and insert to help you understand my experience today.

The Port picture just below is the aerial view of the site.

Next page is another picture of the Port, where I had to maneuver through specific sections, follow signs which allow or direct or prevent access, with workers busy in some places and other places quite empty except for trucks, trailers, and other transportation gear. An awesome place to deliver goods!

I was directed on the yellow routes to "Ports America Outer Harbor Terminal," the blue area at left of this map.

Port of Oakland Maritime Facilities

The outgoing meat loads I bring are for one of its five container terminals. When they said where to park to unload me, they didn't tell me to go to another place so people can unplug the cord before they take containers. I was told to go between 5-6 along the fence, then the truck driver is to listen to the pickup trucks when they come by.

My load was taken off by a rolling crane, stacked up before going on the ship. They plug it in to keep the meat frozen just like I had it.

When they took the container, they ripped the electrical cord. Again, a maze to drive out of the Port. Hope my next delivery is like May 26th, not June 3rd.

Even with a map of the Port, there are so many ways for a truck driver to get lost.

This past April the Port of Oakland exported 84,000 containers, and imported 72,000. About 75% of Oakland's trade is with Asia. It is so huge and the traffic routes and controls and check points are easily confusing until one is very experienced after many deliveries or pickups of the containers.

My delivery went amazing smoothly. I was out of that complex in just thirty minutes. Job finished. But when I got to the Port of Oakland early morning of June 3rd, my experience was *horrible*.

--o-o-o-o-o--

Afternoon:- No load until tomorrow. At Gustine now, and going for the night over to Lodi, north of Stockton, closer to American Canyon and Napa for wine pickups.

June 4 - To Sparks, NV, for the night with only 10 minutes to spare of legal DOT drive time.

June 5 –Made it for the night to Tooele, 30 miles before Salt Lake City, with 30 minutes left on DOT drive time.

Contrast the Port complex with my snap on the next page of the wide open mountainous land around Tooele, Utah, each with its own beauty of scenery and interesting space. Both seen by me in about 30 hours!

79

June 6 – U.S. Route 40 via Heber City, took my noon 30 min. rest at Dinosaur National Monument just barely into Colorado, then by Vail, through the very long Johnson Tunnel, Loveland Pass, STEEP down-hill 6% grade on which I have to down-shift to 5th with the Jake break on in order to slow to 45 mph, and finally for the night at TA Truck Stop in Wheat Ridge, just west of Denver.

June 7 – Driving north, through patches of very dense fog, showers, sun, lovely clouds, then west on I-80 from Cheyenne, Laramie, then Elk Mountain near Rock River, and staying tonight at Little America Travel Center, in Wyoming, I made it here with 41 minutes to spare. Good night everyone. Just 68 miles to Utah, then Oakland here I come!

This morning I was told to drop container at the company yard in Commerce City as the load doesn't deliver until Monday. They gave me another load to pick up at the same that is going to Port America in Oakland by Monday at 7 a.m. I won't make it at that time. I'm on "forced dispatched," which means I have to accept every load they give me. I'm still trying to figure out how they are going to send me home next Wednesday the 11th. I'm guessing I will pick up an empty container to take to the Colton yard.

I realize that to do this job I have to be physically fit, alert,
 eat properly, and get sufficient sleep. "Physical Requirements to Be a Truck Driver" is a comment worth reading, online at Trucker Lifestyle. I walk to the truck stop store, and around the truck stop. My parents urge me to do more. They are correct, but fitting it into driving is a real challenge. With my knees hurting as they get stiff sitting for ten hours (which is equal to 100 miles), I should get out very two hours and walk around the truck ten times.

June 8 – At West Wendover, just inside Nevada, for lunch. Late afternoon, I made it 2/3rds way across Nevada to Imlay, with 55 minutes to spare. Must deliver this load tomorrow around noon. Then I hope I can go home. I miss my things. Going to sleep, very tired.

June 9 early afternoon - Waiting in line at Port of Oakland to deliver this load, but my time is running short. No loads going to southern California, so it looks like I can't go home until this load is delivered and that I get a new load for home...ugh! Running out of hours to drive. DM told me to go to the Oakland yard for the night and deliver in the morning. She is driving me crazy! Now she wants me to go back to the Port to deliver when there are 100 trucks waiting to get in.

At six PM 2 miles from Port, the line inside is too long and I'm running out of time. CRE shares a lot two miles from the Port for parking containers and some trucks stay overnight in this yard. I'm parked in the Oakland drop yard until morning, then deliver the load to the Port.

CRE won't permit me to go home just yet. They are messing with my job schedule. They promised that I would get home after 6 weeks out, yet I'm not getting it – for the second time.

The 'home time' is the first issue that troubles me. Full time CRE drivers are eligible for vacation after they have been employed for 1 year and average 7000 miles a month. The amount is calculated by taking the last 52 weeks of checks and averaging. Secondly, the insurance that is paid from my driving income turned out not to be applicable for three health issues I've faced. Thirdly, the job should pay over $1000 a week and I'm lucky to get 1/4 of it.

That leads me to conclude that I'm done with this company. I will pay CRE off for the $3,000 cost of the schooling. When I get to Colton tomorrow, I'm taking everything that is mine out of the truck. It is too bad to leave a job I love with such a bad taste in my mouth for the company that is using me in ways I dislike.

Twisten has explained that C.R. England (and perhaps many others) has a good business scheme in which they obtain hundreds of students, all school costs paid for by a Federal loan, and the students are then put on the road to earn 11 cents a mile to repay the loan over a period of many months.

Some students believe they're skimped on benefits, many feel done out of what seems proper pay, and quite a few feel cheated out of home time given the "forced dispatch" feature of the driver's contract.

Quite a number of students believe CRE is run deliberately to make working with them unpleasant due to such issues as the three above, so the "students" will quit before they have completed the required months to repay the schooling cost. The company seems to market itself very well to people wanting this type work, stays within the legal bounds of managing its drivers, and thus gains Federal funds and the money that the drivers will "earn" before their time is up – which in my case would have been July 20th.

I conclude it's better to walk away from CRE and move on with my life, perhaps driving for a different company. I'm reminded of what I wrote in chapter 3 about drivers within some months leaving the company due to feeling cheated of home time and health care, to say nothing about being paid "student" wages and less than State laws.

Trucking gets some people to create posters, quotations, comic images, and the imagery. Humor goes on all the time – serious, humorous, bawdy, belligerent, comical, etc.

Here is one poster that caught my eye - since I have always liked cats and my parents had a series of cats in the house as I was growing up on Lathrop Drive, Stanford University, near Palo Alto. We had several other pets!

June 10 mid-morning- I'm in the Port of Oakland, got unplugged the genset cooling (electrical generator system for loads needing climate control), then had the container unloaded off the chassis. It went a bit better today, still got lost inside the Port area. Out in 4 hours, then to get empty container on my chassis. Colton tomorrow.

June 11- Dropped trailer and truck #59161 off. Twist told me to "pull into the Temp Trans yard, turn around, honk the horn, and back up to the empty dock. Walk to safety office and sign your papers." I asked, "What about my test drive?" He said "Parking the truck at a dock shows your driving skills." I did as he said.

Home time! I moved all my things into my Ford Escort. Truck # 59161 had 226,242 miles already on it when it was assigned to me, ending with 280,874 – for total miles driven of 54,632. It means that I've driven across the country from coast to coast the equivalent of eighteen times during this period.

At 30 cents per mile as solo driver, that comes to $16,389 earned. Besides health insurance coming from this sum, a portion has gone to pay off the US loan for truck school. The school loan would be paid off in July. If I leave CRE before then, I need to pay CRE the full school cost. Given all factors, I opt to pay the $3,000.

--o-o-o-o-o--

A Toby Keith song *"Shut Up and Hold On"* was a favorite of my trainer Randy and me. We would crank up the volume when this song came up. Here is a small sample of the lyrics:

Get in, Sit down, Shut up, and Hold on
Can't wait. Too late. It's time to get gone
Find us a dirt road get a groove on
Get in, Sit down, Shut up and Hold on ...

The open road is a pleasure, seeing so much of the country and its varied sights, including remarkable weather and storm patterns. Here is a typical western highway scene.

Here is what my "home time" week gave me time to accomplish. I've unpacked all my stuff from my car. Next, washed my car! Laundry done, unpacked, and then repacked, made food, enjoyed the peace of being at home.

Plus I've called an attorney about the medical benefits that I'm paying for but don't have. (see entry on the pay statement of June 2014, for I had to drive from Reno to Florida before the company permitted me to see a doctor – and was told there that my insurance does not cover what I needed.)

I'll write out that I should have a month vacation due to a temporary arthritic condition in my knee, which then hopefully will require CRE to give me a month off driving. Hope this works out that way.

COMPENSATION SUMMARY	CURRENT	Y-T-D	TAX DEDUCTIONS	CURRENT	Y-T-D
TAXABLE COMPENSATION	366.24	4011.25	FEDERAL TAX	34.74	443.97
LESS PRETAX DEDUCTIONS			STATE TAX	4.08	65.55
HEALTH INSURANCE	35.10	140.40	FICA	20.53	240.00
HSA INSURANCE			MEDICARE TAX	4.80	56.12
401K PLAN			DISABILITY TAX	3.66	40.12
ROTH					
NET TAXABLE COMPENSATION	331.14	3870.85	UNEMPLYMNT TAX		
PLUS NONTAX PER DIEM					
TOTAL NET COMPENSATION	331.14	3870.85	TOTAL TAXES	67.81	845.76

June 27th message to family: Just so you know, I'm on leave from CRE. They are waiting for me to get my insurance back so I can see the doctor.

Chapter 6 – Team Driving for Temp Trans

In 2014, mid-June, I got the call from Temp Trans (TT) with yard in Adelanto, near Victorville on the I-15, over the hills from San Bernardino. I start working on 20th. I have to go to the office and watch a few videos before I get on the road. I'm excited for my new job driving as a team with Twisten.

June 18 - Work in the morning with a better job company. I need 9 months with the company to pay off my driving school loan. I've got previous experience driving commercial, as I was a school bus driver and now upgraded it for 18 wheels. My truck will be a 2012 Freightliner

sleeper, red color, #2004, 13 gears, not the 10 speed I'm used to.

In two hours, Twisten has taught me how to drive 13 gears with an extra switch for the thumb plus the finger switch. The 10 speed only has one switch for fingers.

June 19, a Thursday - I have to make two runs to the east coast before I can take time off to move, plus give the Arroyo Grande apartment landlord a 30-

day notice. Finished filling out TT paperwork and watching videos. Truck is used, new for this company, with passenger seat broken, the bed is sunken and lumpy. No containers to haul. We pull a regular 53-foot trailer, using 5th wheel to turn the trailer which stays locked in place with the kingpin. Is being worked on, oil changed, fuel filter, etc.

June 20 – Now rolling from Victorville on a run above Bakersfield by evening. I drove 123 miles today working the gears. We didn't make it to our pick up before 6 p.m., so we pick up onions and potatoes in the morning. Usually we'll run about 650-675 miles each day.

June 21 – We stop for a tourist's visit to London Bridge (pic by bridge) and an ice cream treat at Lake Havasu City,

June 22, noon, stopping in Albuquerque - Time for a bit of breakfast while my dear man sleeps. I've been driving all this morning. We passed the Cadillac Ranch sculpture in Amarillo; east, in Groom, TX, saw the largest Christian Cross in western hemisphere and its related outdoor sculptures.

June 23 - Passed Little Rock, on to Nashville, as I drive until near midnight at Knoxville, Tennessee, when we swap and Twisten takes the wheel.

June 24 early evening - Philadelphia crossing into New Jersey, and I visited with my long-time Stanford campus friend Bonnie Veaner, meeting at New Jersey Turnpike South Bound, in Edison near New Brunswick, NJ.

June 25, early morning - Good morning Jersey people. Made my pick up on time. Then Twisten and I go to New York and then back to Jersey to swap trailers, to Pittsburgh for lunch, and to Milwaukee by tomorrow morning. I add at noon:- I have been up since 4 a.m.; went to bed 3 hours earlier. Getting lost in what should have been New Jersey, but ended up in New York ... thanks GPS. Got the pick up on time anyhow. Then I wasn't allowed to back the trailer up this morning. Twisten wanted to back it in.

Got to our next pick up in New York, now back in New Jersey again to a dock for this one pallet (with help from Twisten, since I didn't dock it right). We still have to drop this trailer and pick up our old trailer before we can eat. I'm just very tired ... and hungry, so nothing will go right without good rest and food. Crazy morning.

Here again mid-evening, we made it nearly to Pittsburgh, switching drivers. His turn to drive – in the constant stormy rain. My turn now to sleep.

June 26 – Heading west. Late afternoon time to eat at Petro Travel Plaza in Rochelle, Illinois. Twisten says my meal was "PORK Ribs, pulled pork, Dirty Rice mixture MAC 'N CHEESE, Chocolate Brownie, Chocolate pudding, Chocolate Cake and a glass of water because she is watching her figure. I missed the rest of what she ate. I had to Blink. 'Sorry, Twisten, you are wrong. I had chicken, ribs, wild rice, carrots, mushrooms, a bite of chocolate cake that I thought was something else, then you told me where the brownie was and had a bite of that and some chocolate pudding, washed it all down with water.' Anyway, it was good!

89

June 27 - We started out with a schedule that I would be driving midnight to noon, as first shift, and second shift would be noon to midnight. This trip I take the midnight shift. Next trip after my day off I get the noon shift -- by Twisten's orders!

We are in Illinois at the moment waiting to get loaded with Sentient Flavors (natural flavor extracts for Dryers ice cream). Next pickup will be Sensory Effects in Brentwood, MO, with both shipments going to Dryers in Bakersfield, CA. (Dryers Bakersfield has space for a 120,000ft² -20°F freezer ice cream warehouse, six ice cream production lines, and a 20-door shipping dock for trucks.) Late afternoon,

was told the shipment is not for Bakersfield but to the Temp Trans yard in Adelanto. Shipments are on wooden pallets, so we'll drop them for another trucker at the yard. (This is pic of truck-trailer link.) West of St. Louis in mid-evening, the sun has set, and we're getting uploaded as my co-driver is sleeping. Down the Oklahoma mountain toll roads. Next stop is Joplin for a late supper and the next driver change.

For your info, no more hauling containers of 40-foot ones. We haul a 53-foot trailer. The sad thing is it's a company truck which is governed to 60 mph to save money on fuel. When Twisten was hired to TT, they gave him an owner-operator truck that isn't governed at 60, but at 72 mph. When I got signed on to the company, they put Twisten and me in a company truck.

That means we have a "pre-pass" box that lets us go through scales (unless it beeps red), and we don't have to pay tolls out of pocket. (With an owner-operator truck we'd have to pull into every scale, and pay tolls out of pocket, then get reimbursed in our next check.)

June 28 – I drove through Missouri until midnight, and then Twisten took over. Noon - we stop at Cherokee Trading Post in western Oklahoma, and watch longhorn cattle.

June 27 - We started out with a schedule that I would be driving midnight to noon, as first shift, and second shift would be noon to midnight. This trip I take the midnight shift. Next trip after my day off I get the noon shift -- by Twisten's orders! We started out June 27 with a schedule that I would be driving midnight to noon, as first shift, and second shift would be noon to midnight. This trip I take the midnight shift. Next trip after my day off I get the noon shift -- by Twisten's orders! Early

91

afternoon – drivers switch. Now it's my turn in the hot seat. His turn to sleep, with curtain drawn. Midnight changed drivers - in Albuquerque.

June 29 – Back to Barstow on the I-15. Just got the truck washed and a free BBQ too at A & B Desert Truck Stop. (This is Barstow CA picture, on our first cross-country drive of food ingredients.) From here it's less than an hour to TT yard in Adelanto where we drop the trailer.

First roundtrip to the east coast finishing up on our 10th day. It has been a rough week with new things to learn, like doing log books, writing down mileage from start to drop, across state lines, where we fuel up, and switch drivers. Now one day off.

Temp Trans LLC
truck #2004
on our 1st east coast run.

July 1 – Tuesday back on the road after day off, going for a pickup of oranges and grapefruit in Tulare, heading to Philly on this shipment run. Twisten driving until midnight when I took over. July 2nd, I started driving at midnight:- Anyone up who will talk to me all night? At six am, in Winslow, AZ, I'm on my "lunch break" at breakfast time. Twisten is sleeping. I get off work at noon. Nearing Gallup, New Mexico. It's my bed time.

July 3 - Now I am back to driving, at McDonald's, Emporia, Kansas. This evening nearing St Louis, I got sick from a meal at a TA truck stop on I-70 in Wright, MO. I think the cook dropped my steak where it landed on egg shell that I ate. Tried to eat a few Tums to settle my tummy. That didn't work. Luckily at a Walmart, I ran to the bathroom and threw up. Twisten gave me the night off from driving so I could sleep.

July 4 –I'm fine now, ready to roll, entering Indianapolis, then on to Columbus. A bit west from Columbus we stopped to see Misty and Rachael, and Donna whom I have met a few times on the road, and we all went to a Texas Roadhouse in London, Ohio. Twisten knows lots of people across the states as he's been a driver for over 30 years. (We wanted to be in Philadelphia for the 4th of July as it is the biggest and best place for fireworks. Since our first drop was in Denver, PA, and our drive time would not allow us to be there, Twisten made arrangements for us to be there in London, so we could be with friends on the 4th.) We then went to an Amish Pennsylvania Dutch market and bought a few things to eat on the truck, like fruit, lunch meats, drinks, plus the best tasting bread made with egg and onion. Near midnight, we saw some fireworks in Ohio, and spent a few hours sleeping in the parking lot. We have been driving since 10 p.m. and shall deliver part of our load in the morning at 6 a.m.

July 6 – Our first stop is off the I-76 in Denver, PA, done, as I was asleep, by Twisten at the Supervalu Distribution Center. The second drop this morning was at Philadelphia Wholesale Produce Market at 6700 Essington Ave, in Philadelphia. Twisten was in the men's room when I had to park the truck and trailer at the dock. It was a tight fit to back in between two trucks. After I tried twice to do it myself, the third time another truck driver helped me park the trailer.

This facility is publicized as a resource for high quality fresh produce serving customers within a 500 mile radius. Home to 26 merchants, PWPM's cold chain is preserved by 224-sealed dock doors that surround the building perimeter. This design allows the market's entire loading dock and sales floor to be kept at 50 degrees F. all day, each day of the year. With trailers snug against weather-tight loading dock seals, produce moves across the cool loading dock to or from refrigerated warehousing. Now we turn around, heading West, first stop is Indiana, after going through four tunnels in PA – the Allegheny Mountain tunnel entrance being one.

July 7 – We were on hold here in Ohio, experiencing heavy rain and thunderstorms, lighting too. Below is picture of our truck in the rain storm as we take shelter and snap a photo, at the Petro truck stop in New Paris.

Just heard early afternoon we are heading to Affton (just southwest from St Louis), then to Dallas - both for Dryers ice cream flavors.

July 8 at night and very early morning - Wind is pushing us around, with a marvelous lightning show from left to right of the windshield. It's almost dancing to the rhythm of the music that is playing on the Sirius XM radio. We're driving through Illinois. I'm in the passenger seat while watching this storm.

Around noon:- Saw a roll-over on the I-44 east bound in Sullivan, MO, a white truck on its side. Cranes at mile

marker 235 working on it. Road is backed up for miles.

This evening we had a fine Chinese buffet dinner, then rolling on the road again. Reminds me we've had quite a few great meals. One was at the Route 66 Casino off the I-40 just west of Albuquerque. Another was Little America in Cheyenne off the I-80. The *best* ever for me was Rainbow Casino on the I-80 in Wendover NV (see previous pic) which has superb Mongolian BBQ as well as a buffet. In that great restaurant you pick out the frozen foods you want and they cook it on a drum right in front of you - and the service there is great. The *worst* one is Pancho's Mexican Buffet in Dallas.

July 9 - Shutting this rig down for the night, 2 hours out of Dallas, parking at Chacktaw Casino in Durant, Oklahoma. By the way, we had the trailer fixed in Texas, because it was leaking oil from the reefer unit. Rear main engine seal was leaking. Had to change gasket service valve 4 bolt, rear oil seal, crankshaft sleeve, and high moisture dryer. This all came to $787.39 with parts and labor. And mechanics ran our unit through all operations, showing it now is working okay.

July 10 - At Cadillac Ranch again, better then 1/2 way home. We will be home tonight for a late dinner. WHAT CHA' MAKING? But then early this morning, switched drivers and I find the regen won't take, so I have to keep pushing the "override" button every three minutes. Must do this so we can get this truck back to the Temp Trans yard to have it fixed...ugh! (If the engine is not burning properly, then regeneration of soot builds up, the engine gets clogged up, and the engine shuts down unless the RPMs are kept above 1600 for a period of time. So I keep pressing the override button.)

At noon, I did the regen. Now the truck is running without trouble, here in western New Mexico at the Continental Divide on I-40. We had our truck washed while I was sleeping at a place in Barstow called A&B Desert Truck Stop. Twisten parked us at Tehachapi.

July 11 - My turn to drive this morning. I got up at 8:30, did my pre-trip, and started rolling. We didn't have to be in Tulare until at least 11 a.m. By noon I had made it to our

95

drop in Tulare, which was chocolate candy from Kerry Ingredients in Afton, MO (Kerry being an Irish company manufacturing food ingredients and flavors). Also cookie dough and cocoa ladyfingers from Dallas. Both delivered to Dryers (its Tulare publicity:- "Dreyers Grand Ice Cream is in the Food Preparations, N.E.C. industry in Tulare, CA. This company currently has 250,000 employees and a billion $$ in its annual sales.")

Word from TT dispatch told us to go to a Bakersfield mechanic since the regeneration system still gives trouble. Turns out it was a bad sensor. Looks like we don't get to go home just yet, three pick-ups around Bakersfield, namely potatoes and oranges at Big L Packers in Edison, then grapes a bit north at Delano Farms, and carrots at Kern Ridge Growers south in Arvin. Did our first pick up.

Trailer again is leaking oil from the same seal that July 9th was fixed ... not! Truck is just four years old and now has 841,000 miles on it. Thank god we only have to do the pickups and take it to the Temp Trans yard for another driver to take back east. Made it to our second pick up just in the nick of time. We got in at 7:58 p.m. We are the last truck to be loaded. Last stop is 60 miles away and have to be there before midnight. Got it there!

July 12 – Back to Temp Trans terminal yard in Victorville, and lunch with Twisten at Panda Express. I got my first pay as a TT co-driver for our cross-country run June 20-29th.

And Twisten says it is "smaller than most" we shall earn.

It's more than I expected:- 42 cents per mile, split 50/50 between the two of us. For 2nd trip, I will be paid $1,028. (At CRE, I would have to run 3 weeks to get a pay check equal 1 week at TT.)

Never seen this much money in a one-week's check! *I'm so glad I am a trucker.* Weekend off with Twisten at Big Bear City, his home on Big Bear Boulevard, San Bernardino Mountains, at elevation of 6,752 - about an hour drive southeast of Victorville.

Below we are at Stanfield Marsh Boardwalk, at east end of Big Bear Lake.

July 15 – Alas, truck has a leaky main seal, using a gallon of oil per 1000 miles. Not good, so it's in the shop at the yard. When ready, we start up again, same route. Each trip is different, pick-ups are different, but trip is still California to the Philadelphia area and back.

The less time driving for Temp Trans, the less income I receive. So far, it has been much less than promised. For example, we were off work for seven days this week rather than two days. At this point, we will only get 2 round-trips this month rather than 4 in a month. This hurts the pocket book. Consequently Twisten has put on Facebook our invitation for help:-

> *'Trucker Sarah and I are seeking info on a good team Company that runs primarily south of I-40 with work in southern Cal. Anybody out there have any leads? We are ready to jump ship now.'*

Other factors prompt this action: Frank A. Kaiser, owner of this truck, is also the TT Dispatcher who controls job assignments. (There are no Temp Trans trucks, because the trucks are all privately owned and leased to the company.) His truck is not maintained to Federal standards. He turned down the horsepower which is now too weak to get out of a situation if needed. Not good.

Twisten wants us to finish my first true full year of Commercial Trucking on October 17th, and see what our options are at that point. It would be nice to go to a respected company with health and retirement benefits, a reputable company to survive with for the long haul. The quest is on.

July 17 – Finally! Put my travel items in the truck, and got instructions. First pickup in Oxnard at Driscoll's [berries]. Then to Bakersfield region, at Big L Packers [potatoes and oranges] in Edison, third at California Organic Farms in Lamont, and fourth in Arvin at Trino Packing & Cold Storage. (Beyond the 1st pick up, we each earn $10.00 for each additional pickup.) Delivery of these foods this time is

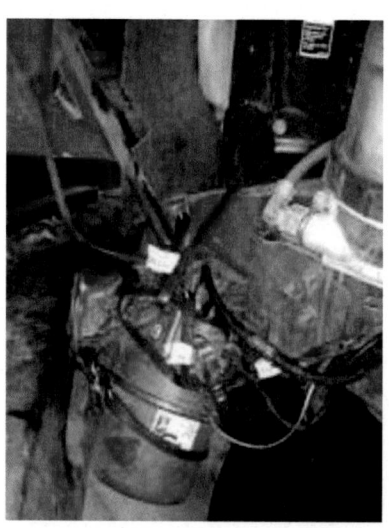

to a different Philadelphia depot: Garden State Farms. That's our trip. But interrupted in the Inner Valley for another breakdown – a broken air dryer, here pictured.

July 18 – The 3rd pick up only had four pallets. Now in Weedpatch, CA, we must go to a scale before the 4th pick, to make sure we can take the extra weight. Total weight of truck and trailer is 80,000 pounds. The steer axle cannot go over 12,000. The driver axle cannot go over 34,000, and same with the tandems.

Then we learned the 4th was cancelled. Our trailer is fully loaded with the truck now carrying a total of 72,760 pounds. All foods, and all on pallets. We head east.

July 20 – Now in Oklahoma, and half way there. We see great cloud formations as we roll through Oklahoma. Yesterday I drove an extra 100 miles (2 hours) to let Twisten sleep. We still have 1,473 miles to go; at 500 per driver, that is three shifts. BTW - I run on California time. Even when I'm in the east coast, my log book remains on California time. Only pickup and deliveries are recorded in local time.

July 21at nearly 2 a.m. - At Flying J truck stop in Carlisle, PA, only 126 miles to go … time to eat. I'm starving. Maybe take a shower before we drop this load off. Went through a few tunnels, tight roads and lots of construction on the roads today. Scared, yet did it!

July 22 – Made it to South Philly on time, now we must wait to unload and reload before heading home. Being late for my father's 90th birthday reminds me of the nitty gritty of trucking. It's a lonely job, where you don't always get to go home to be with family for birthdays or special events. Sure you get to see different places, meet all kinds of people and make new friends across the country. Make good money to do things one day.

It's a hard life when you are by yourself or have a co-driver. You don't get to watch your favorite TV shows. Nor can you plan to go to a party for a family member or friends because you might still be out on the road. There are many car and truck accidents that are minor or deadly. That is the scary part. It's long hours, longer than the average 8 hours a day a person works at a store. It's hurry up to get to the pickups and deliveries. If you're early then you are on time, if you are on time you are late, if you are late, you are better off looking for a different job.

When I get up in the morning, sometimes I don't make it to the bathroom. That is why I have a trash bucket to use if I have to. I have baby wipes to make sure I stay clean. When you fuel up, you get enough points to take a shower, if not then you have to pay out-of-pocket 6 to 15 dollars to take a shower.

Most of the truck stops have fast fried foods, not healthy to eat. That is why a lot of truckers you see are fat. You can't go to a bar after your shift or have a drink or two when your shift is over, like you would at home. You don't have to dress up like in a suit or a dress as you will get dirty. No reason to wear makeup or do your hair, because you don't have to look pretty for anyone but yourself. When I go to a place to load or deliver products I like to look good so that the people remember me, and not just the company I work for. Everyone I meets likes me, so I get treated with respect - as I respect them.

This afternoon on the 22nd, going to Edison NJ to switch trailers, then do a pickup in Northumberland PA for delivery in Wisconsin early day after tomorrow. This is the way our assignment came in:-

> **Trip:0017560 Trailer:53039 - 1)Furmano Foods**
> **770 Cannery Rd Northumberland, Pa 17857**
> **Ph:570-473-4470 PU:5716843D-192cs-9271lbs**
> **7/22/23@7-10fcfs A171883 FCF S Temp:Dry**
> **This load delivers 7/24@10am#6759372**

In other words: After picking up trailer 53039, we are to go to Furmano Foods in Northumberland PA to pick up 192 cases of spaghetti that weigh 9271 pounds. It should have been picked up between 7-10 this evening, but we will pick it up 10 a.m. on Thursday. (We were late for this pick up as I had to deal with Sharon, getting her money and bus tickets to Las Vegas. That is why, when we get this load in the morning, we will have less time to stop and eat.)

I'm listening now to Haydn's Symphony #23 in D Major on my SiriusXM radio. Next pickup in Rochelle, IL.

July 23 - Oh my heavens! How could this happen? We had just gotten off the 76 turn pike in Pennsylvania just a few miles from the Ohio state line. Twisten driving, I'm sleeping, and we have run out of fuel. A man took Twisten to get fuel and starter fluid to start the truck. When we got the truck started, I found out the man who helped us is his father, George! Had lunch with him at King's Family Restaurant in Monroeville, PA, just east of Pittsburgh. Dropped off the Fumono Foods shipment in Menomonee Falls, a village outside of Milwaukee.

July 24 – Now in Rochelle, Illinois, early evening, and tomorrow in St. Louis we shall pick up load at Sensient Flavors (a marketer of colors, flavors, and fragrances; see order next page), this load going to Dryers in Bakersfield CA, for which we haul exclusively when we're heading west July 25 – We're on familiar interstates, with the beauty of some late evening scenes!

```
07/24/14 04.34 PM

PICKUP 7/250 10AM CONF# 748567
SENSIENT FLAVORS
975 S. CARON ROAD
ROCHELLE, IL 61068 (815) 561-8190
*PU# 748567 REF# 4546857033
(19PLTS/ TEMP.40/ 40,535LBS)
FOR: US COLD- BAKERSFIELD, CA
```

July 26, at 12:30 a.m. - Twisten slept from noon to midnight, while I drove. Twisten now driving from midnight to noon. I made it to Kansas, covering 541 miles today, driving twelve straight hours, with two potty breaks.

No scale house ("chicken coop" as we call the DOT scales where officers make sure we are NOT over legal weight). When we weighted our load, we were at 12,320 on the steer axle (can't be over 12,000), drive axle is 30,060 (can't be over 34,000), and tandem's axle is 31,620 (can't be over 34,000). We are over 320 pounds on drive axle.

101

By my driving 500+ miles, we are at legal weight. But it's been a *horrible* day of driving, nonstop because there was not one truck stop on this route, lots of hills, narrow roads, more hills, using all the truck gears. Wish we'd been on the I-70!

Took great pictures of Tucumcari, NM, and the sky over New Mexico. We stopped on West I-40 to look at cars which had been used in movie "Cars."

One other point:- instead of the automatic travel log used by C.R. England trucks, Temp Trans uses a "paper log" of the miles driven in twelve hours multiplied by legal truck speed limit in the state to thus compute the distance in the time interval, keeping the log legal.

Using my Blue Parrot hands-free device connected to my smartphone, I just talked to my father while driving, explaining a few things for my book, and saying I shall be in Albuquerque in 2 hours, Gallop NM by midnight, and then to the TT yard.

Then Twisten takes our load to Dryers (giving me time to go move). I meet Twisten again on the 29th for our next eastern trip. Per usual, it's two weeks on the road which then earns us two days of home time.

July 27, 6:45 p.m. – Got to TT yard. Finished our third roundtrip to the East coast drop and back to the West coast. Turned in my log for payment, which I received. I'm posting a typical itemization on the next page.

Now with help by Tim and a neighbor, move my things out of my Arroyo Grande apartment into a Santa Maria storage unit.

Established in 2008, Temp Trans has 18 trucks, 26 power units, owns 25 Tractors, and has 29 drivers, who drove a total of 3,954,944 miles in 2014. Here below is record of the largest amount earned so far in one month.

Sarah Weber
Unit# 2004
8/1/2014

17518
ADELANTO,CA
OXNARD,CA
EDISON,CA
LAMONT,CA
PHILADELPHIA,PA
EDISON,NJ
17560
EDISON,NJ
NORTHUMBERLAND
MENOMONEE FALLS,WI
17589
MENOMONEE FALLS,WI
ROCHELLE,IL
BAKERSFIELD,CA
5963miles X .21=$ 1252.23+$ 50(5stop)=$ 1302.23

TOTAL
$ 1302.23
+$34.01(reimbursements)
$ 1336.24
-$ 410.00(advances)
$ 926.24

103

A sign seen many a time heading East.

Chapter 7: –
Shifting SNA Gears

Previous chapter finished our third cross-country trips as TT team drivers. This chapter will include exceptional events and surprises of our "team driving" trips from California to the East coast and back. This will run until October, when I shall have been a commercial truck driver for a year. Life is an adventure and I'm living it!

July 30, 2014 – Twisten picked up organic food produce in Watsonville, also at three places in Salinas. Then July 30th, I met Twisten in Bakersfield at his Doctor's, and it's amazing how your doctor will meet you at a truck stop at that hour of the morning on little more than a phone call and a chuckle. I handed in my third trip log today, so will get paid by check upon return to the yard after this fourth trip is complete. We are both very tired. He drove all weekend and Monday and Tuesday to get the loads, while I drove 6 hours home from my yard, paid bills and got my apartment packed up, and then drove 6 hours back to get on the truck.

July 31 – Just inside New Mexico, I stopped for fuel, when I heard of a FedEx trailer on fire at m/m 60 on the 40. Plus lightning and much nasty rain up ahead.

I want to explain the hours of service that a truck driver has. This is complex. Even if I've touched upon it in an earlier chapter, these US Department of Transportation regulations (in my words) control our lives on the road. Here goes -

You have 70 hours of driving for 8 days. A driver drives 11 in a 14 hour window per day. Once you hit 70 hours on the

8th day you must shut down for 34 hours that must include two mornings of 1-5. Then you have your 70 back. So it is best to shut down at midnight to start your 34 hour restart, and one must shut down before midnight, like11:58 p.m. not at the midnight mark. If done any earlier you lose time. This is the part that is confusing to all newbies. As a driver you have 11 hours in a 14 hour window to drive that day. So if you drive as a team it's best to have a schedule like we have, midnight to noon and noon to midnight for the second driver.

If you drive solo and you start driving at 6 a.m., you have until 8 p.m. to finish your drive day. If you stop at a customer at 4 p.m. and they don't finish loading or unloading your trailer until 8 p.m. you can't move anywhere even if you put yourself on off duty that whole time.

You have a special occasion that you can use only once within 7 days that gives you an extra 2 hours more of driving, if you can make that run with your normal time. And an act of God, like stopping for a fatality. If it is posted like the workers are blasting a mountain and it falls on the road you are driving and you can't get to a safe place (like a truck stop or rest stop) over your drive time, you will get written up for DOT violation. In order to have rollover hours it is best to shut down after 8 and a quarter hours. So you can keep driving every day and never having to shut down for a 34 hour restart. Or you can drive your 11 hours and be shut down for 2 days in some place without food, water, and restrooms. So it's best to find a good place to take your 34 hour restart where you might get to see new things - like Niagara Falls. Now all clear?

--o-o-o-o-o--

August 2 - Dropped our last load in Rochester. Swapped drivers...that was a short day for me to drive today. To Niagara Falls, my first time, and for Twisten also.... I only dream that I would get to visit these places, but I get to see it today. *An amazing place, just marvelous!* Twisten and I placed a number of pictures on our Facebook pages for

106

friends. Here is one overview seen early evening, and the other is of the "team drivers" taking their well-earned break.

The "American Falls," a fraction of the totality of Niagara Falls, includes the Horseshoe Falls on the Canadian side and smaller Bridal Veil Falls in the U.S.

Even in the late evening one finds large groups of people visiting the overlook to see the color in the mist from the falls beyond which are the lights of the city of Niagara Falls. Located on the Niagara River, which drains Lake Erie into Lake Ontario, the combined falls form the highest flow rate of any waterfall in the world, with a vertical drop of more than 165 feet.

August 4 – We both hope to go to SNA Transportation Inc., with main offices in Rancho Cucamonga CA and New Bethlehem OH. Twisten found it on the back of one of the trucks passing us. He called them up and told them about us. When we get back, they want us in this week to give them our DMV printout and take the drug test. We get 50 cents per mile, more then what we are getting now. Plus drive a new Peterbuilt or Kenworth. My bus driving for 2 1/2 years, upgraded with a Class A, gives me 3 years of commercial driving experience.

August 5 - We just spent the last 2 hours at the TA in Strafford, MO, getting our truck worked on. The condenser for the Air Conditioner went out 2 days ago. We have been sweating like crazy due to the humidity. Finally got the truck back, so we're rolling. To St Louis for Kerry Ingredients pickup, then into Oklahoma headed to So Cal, then flipping back to Philly, Minnesota, Rochelle Illinois, and home again to Victorville TT yard to drop truck and load on the 7th.

August 8 – Bad news: SNA said I needed two full years commercial driving before they would accept us for team driving. We shall continue to watch for alternatives. I posted on Facebook to 'Heavy Truck Fans and Drivers'-

"Howdy friends, I've been driving for a year and my team driver has been driving 33 years. We are looking for a dedicated run that goes on the I-40 south on states. From California to Florida, maybe the Carolina's. We are out of Southern Calif."

108

Two days later: SNA phoned me to say it would accept me if I pass a driving test, which I plan to take after one more Temp Trans roundtrip to east coast.

Transportation Inc.

August 13 – Deliveries and pickups are the routine. Today we pick up one pallet from upstate New York in Congers.

On the 14th - No new orders yet. And it's only 5:35 a.m. California time. I hope in a few hours they will have our next pickup orders. I'm tired and I have to wait until noon time at home before I can go to sleep. But for now I'm watching the leaves fall from the wind in Congers, NY.

August 15, been on the go since early morning. Now at Edison, NJ, and, oh my goodness, this Edison Diner is better than any diner I've been in. Twisten had first meal of the day here, seared shrimp. It's a 5-star restaurant. The food is fabulous, staff awesome. Love this place.

We were told to go to four other pickups but once we got there, all four had been picked up by another driver for our

company. Making us run around for 2 days. On the way to Kraft Foods pickup (a full load) in Walton, New York, we drove through lovely Pennsylvania back country, off the major highways. Here is a sample scene of this rural region – totally beautiful country.

When we were told to pick up Kraft, it was a full load of "refrigerator products" going to a drop in Ontario, CA. I was upset that we wasted two days to find out that the loads are already gone.

August 16 –Evening in Missouri was so dreadfully scary – lightning bolts all around. Heavy heavy rain in downpour. I slowed way down, put my hazard lights on. At last I was beyond it all – but what an experience.

Twisten steers us to the Big Texan Steak Ranch for our dinner – and tablecloth! – a famous spot on the I-40 in Amarillo, TX. (See snapshot.)

August 18 - Good night, my friends. I drove all night. This gal is dead tired. I'm going to sleep now, at Kingman, AZ. Evening at Barstow's A&B Desert Truck for a wash.

August 19 – Well, this morning I woke up in the truck, ready for my test drive for the new company. I can do this. YES, I GOT THIS. Time to get into my car and head over. Than tonight we drop this load.

Later:- I took SNA driving test and passed! We are 'IN' - yeah! Two more east-coast trips with Temp Trans and then we plan to sign on as team drivers with company SNA in Rancho Cucamonga, near Ontario, CA.

August 20 - I'm back at the Temp Trans yard, the load was to be delivered tonight at 7:45 p.m. local time, but the customer said it was to be delivered at 7 p.m. (My company didn't give that information to me.)

Plus I had to refuel the truck when I arrived, since someone took the truck out somewhere yesterday, when they should have fixed the oil leak. Had to call boss about it, and he was not pleased. Looks like I'm staying in Adelanto, CA, for the night alone.

As Twisten says, *"Let's get this show back on the road. Only two more flips before we jump ship to new company. At SNA. we have a choice of either an older truck with a 13-gear speed, or a new truck that is a 10 speed. Thinking of getting the 10 speed truck."* Twisten said it's my choice.

August 28 – working our way west. At 6 am, I sweet-talked the highway officer to get out of a speeding ticket.

Late morning, I'm in so much pain in both my knees I just want to cry...but that won't stop the pain. I've got to drive as far as I can today, because morning I deliver this load. I wish I had pain pills, but I will be using the patches, knee braces and my cane to get around. So hold the door for me so I can waddle into the bathroom or get a bite to eat.

A bit later, midway on the I-76 Pennsylvania Turnpike, we drove close to the site where 40 heroic passengers and crew, by only 18 minutes, forced the crash and thereby saved the US Capitol from destruction.

This site is marked now by the National Memorial to recognize the hijacked United Airlines Flight 93, where the airplane crashed in a field by Shanksville, PA. We had a visit to the site of this remarkable event. The explanatory colored plaque I insert on the next page was part of the Memorial explanation.

111

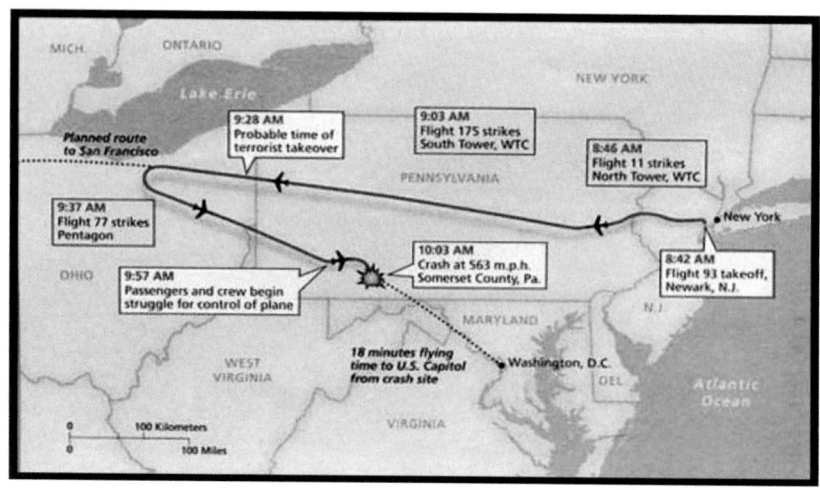

Map showing flight paths with the following labels:

MICH. ONTARIO

Lake Erie

NEW YORK

Planned route to San Francisco

9:28 AM Probable time of terrorist takeover

9:03 AM Flight 175 strikes South Tower, WTC

8:46 AM Flight 11 strikes North Tower, WTC

PENNSYLVANIA

9:37 AM Flight 77 strikes Pentagon

10:03 AM Crash at 563 m.p.h. Somerset County, Pa.

New York

OHIO

9:57 AM Passengers and crew begin struggle for control of plane

8:42 AM Flight 93 takeoff, Newark, N.J.

N.J.

MARYLAND

WEST VIRGINIA

18 minutes flying time to U.S. Capitol from crash site

Washington, D.C.

DEL

Atlantic Ocean

VIRGINIA

0   100 Kilometers
0   100 Miles

August 29 - Ugh! I just want to go home...but then I realized I am home...I live on the truck. In pain but gotta roll on. The pain is my knees both hurt at the knee cap area. Can barely walk without a cane. My knees give out on me, and buckle under me. Makes it hard at times to use the clutch, fuel and brake. Plus my wrists are in a lot of pain because I have carpal tunnel syndrome in both wrists, when it's windy it's hard to hold on to the steering wheel.

Since knees are more essential than wrists, I lost weight for my knees, to postpone the surgery a bit longer, for the doctor says I'm too young to get the knees done. They want me to be 60 years old before that.

We are doing a relay in Wyoming. Someone is picking up a loaded trailer and swapping with our load. They are picking up in Salt Lake City and bringing it to us and they will take our load to California.

Oh, now the orders have changed. We are going to Salt Lake...ugh. We take their load to Philadelphia. Then we should be getting another load to California.

Then we clean the truck to turn it in. Very heavy rain in Laramie today, as my snapshot shows.

August 30 – That late afternoon, our compressor went out, no air in the brakes, stranded at Laramie, and I phoned my father asking if he could find us a room. No luck, for a huge football game resulted in all of the eighteen hotels full, so not one room could be found.

We'll have to sleep on the truck in the repair shop.

August 31 in Laramie Wyoming - YES! We are back on the road again. We have a new trailer, and part of our load is going to Salt Lake City, the rest to Bakersfield.

Yet Twisten cautions me: "Don't count your chickens before they hatch. This load had been changed six times in the past 36 hours."

September 1st - We lost our air compressor (to keep up to 130 psi but it was excessive, going up to 160 psi). Everything to do with the air supply system failed except the lines themselves. The load we had was relayed to another truck, and while we were playing 'tourist' games, the owner of the company kept playing hot potato with the trailers.

By the time our truck was ready to roll, the trailer had six times been "changed out," swapped. We got back on our

original run to Salt Lake City, where today we toured the Mormon Temple (and I took this picture of Thorvaldsen's Christus, an 11-foot statue of the Savior).

No deliveries here today to union shops.

Last run with this slow company. Told our boss today that this is our last run, as we have too many days of down time due to their planning of our loads.

Soon we have a few days off, as SNA wants us to take a few hours of a class that is only given on Monday and Tuesday. Then SNA has for us a new Kenworth truck, with a bigger "apartment sleeper" space, waiting for us on Tuesday or Wednesday to start with a faster truck, 12 days out and 3 days off, and paying 55¢ a mile.

September 2 – Had chance for brief visit with Sharon as we drove through Las Vegas.

On a later run East for SNA, we stopped at a golf driving range in Baton Rouge. Here is a snap by Twisten as I am taking a grip to hit another -- a sample of how we occasionally take a break for our health's sake.

September 3 – Early morning at Nestle Ice Cream Facility, Bakersfield, where we made our last delivery.

Now back to the Temp Trans yard near Victorville. Unload truck, clean it up pretty, and turn in keys. I have been up all day and night. I'm pooped. I'm not done yet. In the wee hours, the only place still open is Applebee's. My new trucking job with SNA can start September 17th.

September 4 – Temp Trans has an offer on the table. They are going to up the speed on the truck to run 65 mph and cruise control at 67, and paying for layovers and break down time. We do like TT. The truck is finally getting all the bugs worked out, so now it won't break down as much. TT is hurting for drivers and is now willing to give us what we ask. So, all things considered, it's reasonable for this established team of drivers to stick with Temp Trans for a while longer.

Ah, the sights seen in this large country!

Chapter 8:–
Very Unusual Loads

The year 2015 was a year of transition. Twisten decided we should leave TT and move to SNA Transportation, with lots located in Fontana and Pomona, CA. He found it a better fit for our home situation, health issues, and needed time off. It has a good reputation.

SNA is the parent of about 25 companies which own and operate big rigs, and the small sub-company we now drive for is called PNS, located in Pomona, CA. We started with PNS in March, and through November 2015 we two 'team drivers' drove 183,000 miles.

We had done several trips to the east coast in this white Freightliner 2015 truck owned by LS Pacific Enterprise of Glendale. This time, in November 2015, we were routed to Lansing, Michigan to pick up a load heading to the west coast. Loaded up an extremely light-weight load filling two-thirds of the trailer and took off to California,

I started driving my shift in Dixon, Missouri, heading west on the Interstate 44 highway at midnight California time. By the time I got to Oklahoma City, Oklahoma, early on Thanksgiving Day of 2015, it was getting lighter, and it started to sprinkle rain. I was looking for the Interstate exit to take us from the I-44 to the I-35, heading to the I-40. About 7 a.m. I got the I-44 off ramp while Twisten was still asleep in the sleeper.

I felt a jolt in the road and I yelled, "*Daddy, hold on we are going to crash.*" I tried repeatedly to correct the direction of the truck (but I over-steered), the truck hit the side rail repeatedly and flipped on its side while sliding across the ramp bridge. I'm still in the driver's seat, still with my seat belted in. Suspended firmly by the belt, I could not move. I just could yell. Twisten had been in bed with curtain drawn, unbuckled, and was bouncing around like a ping pong ball, in the midst of flying debris from the opened cabinets.

I did not feel injured, told Twisten that I was all right. Twisten came up from the back and turned off the truck engine, and asked if I could get out. I said 'no', and he was able to unbuckle me from the seat belt. Helped me down from my seat and I was then sitting on the built-in refrigerator. Everything fell on to the passenger side. Twisten found our very warm reflective safety vests and told me to put it on (this early morning was a chilly 54 degrees) and I put on the vest.

Then I saw a man open the door; he asked if we were alright; he wanted to help us out of the truck. Twisten said, "*Is the truck on fire?*" The man said 'no', then closed the door. Twisten was looking for clothes, and tried to find his phone. Twisten asked me to call his phone from mine, and keep calling it until he found it. I did as he asked, and kept calling every second until he found his phone. I was so scared and didn't know what else to do.

During the time I was calling his phone, the fire department ambulance showed up. The fireman had an axe and yelled *"back away, I'm going to break the window."*

And immediately Twisten told them -- *"No! It kicks out."* But the fireman ignored Twisten, so I grabbed the blanket and covered us with it. The badly-trained fireman broke the glass inwards and helped me out of the truck.

Then I was ordered on to the gurney and taken to the ambulance.

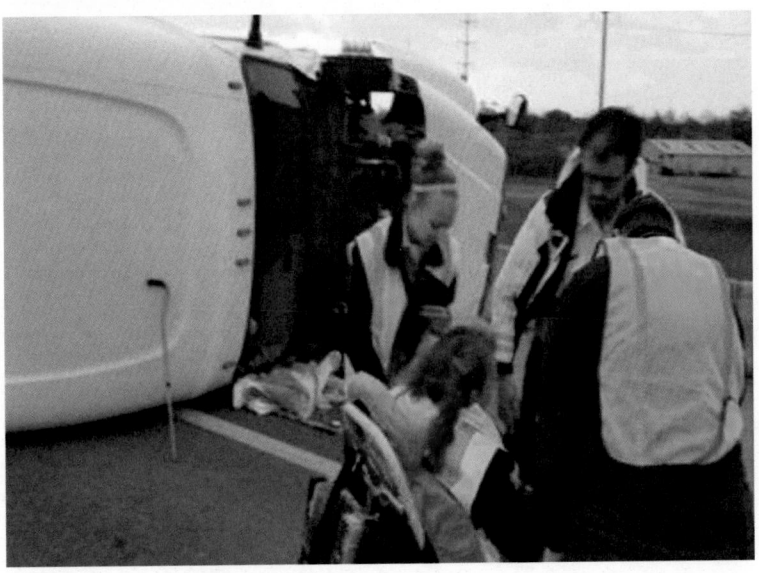

While the ambulance crew members were checking me out, Twisten grabbed the Road Dawg camera he had attached to the passenger windshield, which records for two minutes. Recording time ran out during the accident.

Twisten then used my cell phone to take pictures, and finally used his cell phone when mine ran out of energy.

With light rain still falling, Twisten walked around taking pictures of the aftermath – everything visible, on the road, all parts of the truck and trailer, everywhere, while the ambulance waited 45 minutes for him to finish.

He did a thorough job of it, lots of detailed shots, shots to demonstrate wheel marks, ramp side barrier marks, all damage to truck and the trailer, leakage, fragments of debris here and there, condition of the load on the highway and in the trailer, and the three light posts that were knocked down during the crash.

Westbound I-44 Reopened, Near May In NW OKC, After Semi Rollover

Posted: Nov 26, 2015 7:04 AM PST Updated: Nov 26, 2015 12:52 PM PST

BY MATTHEW NUTTLE, NEWS9.COM EMAIL

Then we both were rushed to the hospital. We had the doctors check us out, taking x-rays. Twisten was on the phone talking to our boss and his son. I was crying as I didn't see Twisten until the tests were done.

Then via the hospital phone, I get a call from Twisten's son Nick asking me if I was all right. I told him I was fine, but more worried about his father. Nick consoled me, saying it was an accident. I was so grateful that he was not upset with me, for I could have killed his father. That was the scariest part of it all.

While we're still at the hospital, the officer called Twisten and told him that there were a total of seven accidents on that same ramp that day. Five accidents were before us and two after us!

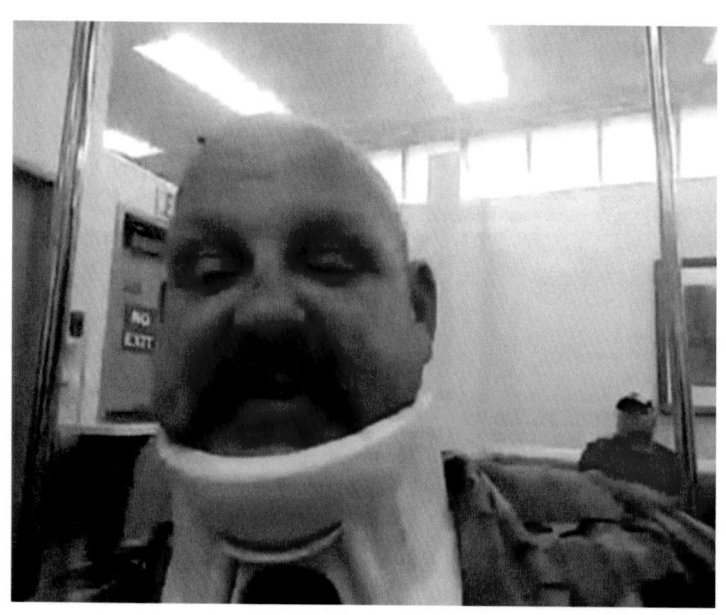

Divot parts of the metal expansion joints on bridge were broken off. (Hard to see in the snapshot inserted below.)

Our very light load combined with weather, slick surfaces, and damaged road conditions caused my losing control.

And the trailer load? The bill of lading only informed us we were hauling "Disney Interactive."

Much later we learned we were transporting boxes of characters in a Star Wars movie, confidential and unknown to us since the movie had not yet been released. (*Episode VII - The Force Awakens* was released l Dec. 18, 2015.) We got some glimpse of the load from the television newscast we saw in our hotel room.

The shipment filled only 2/3rds of the trailer, and was extremely light in weight – just 15,000 lbs. – which meant that strong winds would whip the trailer back and forth. The Michigan load was heading to Stockton, California, for delivery at the Target distribution center.

View of trailer on right side, overhanging the bridge rail.

After the accident, some of the transported boxes were strewn on the highway, as shown above, but most remained in the trailer. Another snapshot on the previous page is one showing broken cartons on the roadway. And the next page has Twisten's picture of the trailer interior seen after the wrecking crew got it back on its wheels.

By the way, most of these pictures of the accident were taken by Twisten – snapped in the drizzle, using our cell phones.

He also took a video, but the few images I've inserted in this chapter are sufficient to illustrate this unfortunate accident and how we survived – with our lives!

After discharge from the hospital, a male Uber driver came to pick us up and take us to a Comfort Inn motel, by the I-40.

We walked slowly to a place to eat next to the hotel, the Cracker Barrel at 700 Cornell Parkway by the I-40.

Then after eating, we walked back to the hotel to watch the televised news, and there we saw our truck and trailer being dragged sideways by the tow truck, all windows broken.

We slept, helped by Advil PM. The next morning we had breakfast at the hotel. Then a female Uber driver Heather picked us up to take us to the wrecking company to gather what we could, and the Uber driver signed off the clock for well over an hour as she helped us get stuff from our truck to put into her car. I got her name and phone number.

Weeks later when we next were in town, nurse Heather was off duty for an hour, met us and gave us what she'd kept in her car for us. She took us to the airport where there were tickets waiting for us to take a flight from Oklahoma to Texas, then another flight to California.

Once we landed in California, Twisten was on the phone with our company, trying to find us another Uber driver to take us home. There were none, but a different company Lyft was found with a driver who gave us both water and took us home.

--o-o-o-o-o--

Time lapse - Now it is December 2015. We had stayed at home for two weeks to recover. Twisten had a broken toe. I had a broken rib, and was sore from head to toe. Twisten was my hero. He told me everything would be all right, he loved me, and he wouldn't let anything happen to us. He still feels safe with me driving while he sleeps.

After the two weeks, we needed to earn money to pay routine bills. So Twisten got us down to the SNA company to see a doctor to get us released for driving, had a meeting with the safety director. The company asked me how I felt about the crash, and whether I felt I could still work. I said if I don't go back working I'm going to freak out and flip out over this mess. I need to drive. I need to go back to that same ramp and 'own it.'

The company talked to each of us separately. They felt I was 'good to go' again. We were given a good used truck. SNA determined I did nothing wrong, and did as anyone should do. Twisten's use of the dash cam saved our jobs.

After a dozen or so trips with PNS (part of SNA), driving loads to and from east coast locations to California pickup or delivery locations, Twisten and I left PNS (scheduled by SNA) to drive for another SNA owner-contractor "Around The Clock" (aka ATC Trucking Co.) - that truck's routes and routines better fit our personal needs and preferences.

Although there are no health benefits with SNA, however we make better money with this firm, and have more home time each flip back to California. Plus I am able to visit my doctor for palliative knee injections.

Our East coast trip April 2016 is a sample of long hauls. We drove out of Pomona, picked up in California, serving a drops first in Allentown, PA, South Windsor, Conn., and another at Billerica, MA, and finally to a drop in Rye, NH.

April 15, picking up a half load in the northeast. When people ask what we're transporting, we tell them "seems they are batteries." Always, Federal law controls the entire load confidentiality during shipment.

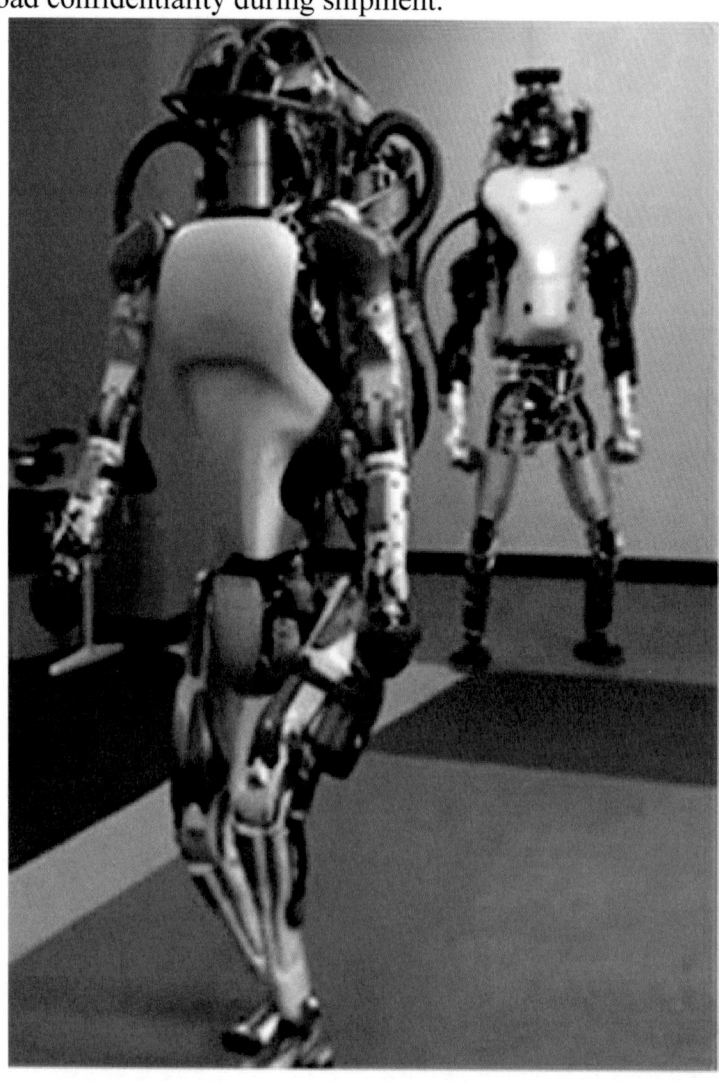

We deliver in two days to a rep at the San Jose Airport. This trip we find out that we're moving four creations by a company specializing in outdoor humanoid robotic variations – different from but akin to the one called "Atlas" made public February in this public announcement:-

"A new version of Atlas, designed to operate outdoors and inside buildings. It is specialized for mobile manipulation. It is electrically powered and hydraulically actuated. It uses sensors in its body and legs to balance and LIDAR and stereo sensors in its head to avoid obstacles, assess the terrain, help with navigation and manipulate objects. This version of Atlas is about 5' 9" tall (about a head shorter than the DRC Atlas) and weighs 180 lbs."

I sent my parents a YouTube video website for them to get a rough idea of something similar to our load. (On previous page is my father's screen grab of an "Atlas" robot.)

When we carried the robots, the load included their batteries and all tools and equipment to control them. Though it was a half load, it was *extremely* heavy. We had a trip paper for each robot, batteries, and equipment.

We seldom know what we're transporting, and almost never is it a product of this awesome nature. SNA relies on our team to move some most valuable shipments, which explains why this westward trip was just half a load. For security purposes, highly confidential loads can't be joined by any other shipment.

April 18 – These fabulous robotic creations would certainly qualify as the most unusual load. Just sit down, get internet connection, go to YouTube, call up robotics or robots, and be ready to be amazed at the various incredible robotic creations in action.

We delivered the four robots to the San Jose Airport, per schedule. We've transported various types of loads - food ingredients, perishable meats, clothing, equipment of all sorts, crates imported and for exportation, building material, (never hazardous products). Now add robots!

Later today, SNA has us picking up in Hayward, CA, a load of cryogenics. But not cryogenics, just a load of brackets, which finally turn out to be complete load of Styrofoam blocks, designed in various shapes so as to carry body organs, packed in the custom-shaped blocks of Styrofoam which we're taking to Pennsylvania.

PS to the Thanksgiving crash:- Twisten was driving on an Oklahoma Interstate interchange months later, experienced same severe trailer swinging due to slick pavement – *very* dangerous conditions. He experienced what I had faced.

Chapter 9:–
Settled in the Routines of
Long-distance Trucking

April 22, 2016 – Pennsylvania delivery made. Fast turn-around, and heading west, now in Tucumcari, NM.

I send my family Facebook word that "It's hot; it's windy as heck. I'm shutting down. Good night everyone. Be safe my driver friends. Sending love to my family." Heading home for a week on our own.

April 25 on Facebook - Well, do I take a week off? Or go on the road solo? (My co-driver will be taking care of family.) On Facebook, Twisten posts:- 'Go solo. She is strong enough. She was trained by the best, to be the best!' But decided we both need time to handle family issues. So we're now on 'home time' and very busy indeed all week.

May 2 - Back on the road for SNA, we transported a load to the Midwest. Then bringing freight of all kinds from Bryan Systems in Montpelier, Ohio, and from JEC Steel Co.,

Goshen, Indiana, for California drops in Riverside, Rancho Cucamonga, Ontario and Stanton.

From California, we take a full FedEx load to Minnesota. Then pick up load there taking it to Maryland. Picking up another load close to the drop and taking it to Georgia, and from there another load via Texas to Anaheim, California, to start our driving break – what amounts to our "Christmas vacation." Well, that break was postponed. We're off again to the East coast.

June 15 - At noon I turn over the wheel to Twisten, in Van Horn, in far western Texas. He was driving west on I-10, by exit 85 interchange, and he saw monster billows of black smoke. We at once agreed to see if the drivers of the truck on fire needed our assistance. The man was driving, with his wife in the sleeper.

Driver rode his breaks going twenty miles down a mountain grade, then realized he had fire so he dropped his trailer, but not quick enough to save the truck. The tractor's tires had caught fire. The fire rapidly spread, truck a total loss for Quest Global Inc. We stopped to help out, and Twisten and I took seven pictures (below picture was in my Facebook posting afterwards).

We used our fire extinguisher, gave the drivers water, food, and a.c. while their truck and trailer were burning. A Twisten rule of the road:- Best on long steep declines to shift into lower gear and have your Jake brake on, so the engine controls speed, not using the air breaks."

Glad to arrive safely in the SNA yard, because in Girard, Ohio, we had to stop for an emergency. Both of us were getting sick from fumes entering the cab. It turned out that three of four batteries were smoking. They were taken out of service; we got home safely using just one.

--o-o-o-o-o--

Thus go the routines on the highways, schedule received from the trucking company dispatcher, driving from the lot to our first pickups, team driving over twenty hours each day, stopping for a meal and gassing up, delivery, proceeding to next pick up and/or delivery, dealing with highway issues, and the weather we are given, day after day after day, the final delivery drop, getting truck and trailer washed and refueled, and back to the company lot. Then in time a welcome break for "home time."

As I wind up the story of my first three years of trucking, a grandmother embarking on a new career, adventures delightful and the miles covered amazing. I've lucked out with this new career. April of 2013 was the start of my schooling. Because of the inferior quality of that school and its truck equipment, I moved to a better school, and in October, with its good instruction, I graduated and had my California Commercial Driver's License to handle big rigs.

So on October 20th of 2013, I drove my truck 502.1 miles on my first day on the job.

A good rule of thumb is 100,000 miles a year for a solo driver. As a team leader, Twisten is a demanding driver (what I lovingly call a "SLAVE DRIVER"), pressing our pace within the constraints of the law and the US DOT. In our four trucks and almost one and a half years currently with this SNA company, we have had trucks driven over 400,000 as well as my 100,000 on the other trucks before stepping out. (Below is our first SNA sleeper tractor.)

I have driven 1/2 of those miles myself. It is hard for me to believe, but - in thirty months while we've worked as a team – Twisten and I have driven the equivalent of 20 times around this earth, at the circumference!

These three years have been stimulating, positive, joyous and challenging for me. I've become a professional driver of a big rig, experiencing a wide range of conditions, a few events bad, most very good, and one extremely dangerous.

This book candidly documents the experiences and times to the best of my ability. As I've said several times - "I love this career." It's like a paid vacation.

My children and their children will always be the most rewarding and dear persons in my life. They are my pride and joy forever and always. It's been great to have "home time" so that every few weeks I can be with them.

I think back fifty years, seeing my life experiences. A picture from back then shows me steering a rented houseboat in the upper reaches on the famous extensive California Central Valley Delta, east of San Francisco.

Times to remember!

Twisten has been mentor, teacher, guardian, supporter – what would I ever do without him! He has been with me as "team driver" and great companion on the adventures covered in the previous chapters. We were married in California on Feb. 29th of 2016 (Leap Year). I'm married to the man I admire and love.

The future looks to be very rewarding. Back on the road, trucking in a big rig, carrying loads near and far. Just an exciting stimulating part of my life story - while Twisten and I 'team drive' far and wide, *Rockin' in a Big Rig.*

Big Bear Lake, by Twisten, during "home time"
between our coast-to-coast trucking runs.

Postscript by My Parents

As a family, we spent a summer on Lake Coeur d'Alene in Idaho. Sarah caught fish and enjoyed boating there and driving up and back over scenic country. We visited relatives in Spokane. We drove around many parts of California. We visited state and national parks. Summers we rented cottages at Echo Lake, and Shaver Lake in the mountains. And by Monterey Bay we stayed at La Selva Beach, Pajaro Dunes, and Seaside.

The countryside, seashores, lakes, and mountains appealed to us all. These escapes from urban routines and chores, these breaks from work, they were our vacations, our 'blue-highway' explorations, freedoms and fascinations.

When Sarah held jobs in stores, filling inventory, stocking shelves, receiving and shipping products, she must have been intrigued by the trucks which delivered and picked up shipments. Further, the activity and chance to be outdoors and to see new interesting places she could feel calling her.

On the highways, massive 18-wheel trucks made an impression on us all. As she has written, Sarah's fascination with trucks started in her late 20's, grew during her 30's & 40's, and sprang into life as she reached 50.

137

Living for half her life in Fresno enabled her to watch the trucking commerce. From the drabness of city life, truck-driving could be a refreshing escape via the adventures of the open road.

Gradually this trucking interest evolved into a fascination. She could visualize a career on the open road.

So as she turned fifty, Sarah deliberately set out to enter this life style. She worked diligently and persistently to qualify and gain the rigorous training required. Her hard work led to this experience, the story here recorded of her career during her first year as a trucker, driving loads coast to coast, and coping with her truck, various pickup and delivery conditions, freight temperature constraints, plus the highways, traffic, and weather.

We admire her very much for settling on a fascinating and demanding occupation, setting a goal, and achieving it – as she now maneuvers a huge heavy truck moving freight nationwide. As parents, it is gratifying to see Sarah enter this satisfying career, to set out to achieve it. And succeed!

How we do admire you, amazing Sarah!

With our love, Mom and Dad

Made in the USA
Middletown, DE
06 August 2016